mini Abu Dhabi

The Ultimate **Visitors'** Guide

In Association With

Abu Dhabi Mini Explorer 2nd Edition
ISBN 978-9948-8584-0-9

Select photographs courtesy Abu Dhabi Tourism Authority
& Abu Dhabi National Hotels Corporation

Printed and bound by
Emirates Printing Press, Dubai, UAE

Explorer Publishing & Distribution
PO Box 34275
Dubai , United Arab Emirates
Phone (+971 4) 340 8805 **Fax** (+971 4) 340 8806
Email info@explorerpublishing.com
Web www.explorerpublishing.com

Introduction

Ahlan Wasahlan... is the Arabic welcome greeting – and Abu Dhabi extends a warm and sincere welcome to all our friends from overseas.

Hospitality is one of the most treasured values of Arabic culture and lies at the heart of our desire to open our doors and welcome international travellers. We believe that tourism can play an important role in promoting friendship, goodwill and understanding and, as the following pages show, Abu Dhabi has a wealth of attractions to fascinate and tempt visitors. The Emirate brings together the ancient culture and heritage of Arabia with cosmopolitan sophistication in a clean and safe environment, offering a distinctive blend of east and west.

Abu Dhabi has always been a special place but, until recently, it remained an undiscovered jewel. Today, more and more overseas visitors are experiencing the magic of this unique and captivating destination.

Sultan Bin Tahnoon Al Nahyan
Chairman

Abu Dhabi Tourism Authority

Head Office
P.O. Box 94000 Abu Dhabi,
United Arab Emirates
Tel: +971 2 444 0444
Fax: +971 2 444 0400
info@adta.ae

Germany
Goethestr. 27
60313 Frankfurt
Tel: +49 172 8857 179
Fax: +49 892 3 662 199
mark.wolter@t-online.de

UK
No. 1 Knightsbridge,
London, SW1X 7LY
Tel: +44 207 201 6400
Fax: +44 207 201 6426
UK@adta.ae

France
11bis rue Blanche
75009 Paris
Tel: +33 1 53 25 03 52
Fax: +33 1 53 25 11 12
France@adta.ae

Contents

Overview

Location

ABU DHABI, THE CAPITAL OF THE UNITED ARAB EMIRATES, IS ONE OF THE WORLD'S MOST PROSPEROUS AND RAPIDLY DEVELOPING CITIES. IN LITTLE OVER HALF A CENTURY IT HAS SEEN A DRAMATIC TRANSFORMATION FROM A SMALL BEDOUIN SETTLEMENT TO A THRIVING BUSINESS AND TOURISM CENTRE OF GLOBAL STATURE.

The UAE sits on the north-eastern part of the Arabian Peninsula, bordered by Saudi Arabia to the south and west and by Oman to the east and north. The country is made up of seven emirates of which Abu Dhabi is by far the largest, occupying over 85% of the landmass. There are two major cities within the emirate: Abu Dhabi, which is the capital of the UAE, and Al Ain west region, which lies at the foot of the Hajar Mountains on the border with Oman.

The island city of Abu Dhabi is a lush, modern metropolis, complete with tree-lined streets, futuristic skyscrapers, huge shopping malls and international luxury hotels. The city is surrounded by the sparkling azure waters of the Arabian Gulf which offer a striking contrast to the large parks and green boulevards that spread across the island. From its origins as a centre for pearl diving and fishing, Abu Dhabi has developed at breakneck speed to become a truly 21st century destination.

Built on a grid system running from a central 'T', the city is easy to navigate. The 'T' is formed by the corniche, which runs along the end of the island furthest from the mainland, and Airport Road which runs the length of the

Weather Report

Perpetual sun and clear blue skies – that's the best way to describe Abu Dhabi's weather. The city has a subtropical, arid climate. Rain is infrequent and, when it does come, showers rarely last long. Temperatures range from a low of around 10°C (50°F) on a winter's night, to a high of 48°C (118°F) in summer. As an island, Abu Dhabi becomes very humid in the hottest months (July, August and September).

island. Roads parallel to the corniche have odd numbers (the corniche is 1st Street) and roads running vertically have even numbers (Airport Road is 2nd Street, with 4th Street, 6th Street, etc. leading off to the east, and 24th Street, 26th Street, etc. to the west).

With much of the interior of the emirate comprising desert, including part of the spectacular Rub Al Khali (Empty Quarter), or sabkha (salt flats), many visitors are surprised by how green the cities are. The combination of high temperatures and inhospitable terrain limits the variety of natural fauna and flora but the Abu Dhabi authorities are working hard to 'green' the urban landscape. Everywhere you look you'll see manicured lawns, pretty flowers and an abundance of palm trees which are maintained by an army of workers.

The cities are known for their beautiful public parks, but even the meridian strips on the miles and miles of highways are oases of greenery. Despite the harsh environment, indigenous nature and wildlife are still worth exploring, with around 1,000 plant species recorded in the

How far?

With the city's modern international airport, getting here is easy.

From	Flight Time (hrs):
Bangkok	6.00
Brussels	6.30
Frankfurt	6.10
Geneva	6.15
Johannesburg	7.45
London	7
Mumbai	2.50
Munich	6
New York	14.30
Paris	6.35
Sydney	14
Toronto (via Brussels)	13.45

(Approximate timings, gate to gate from Etihad Airways)

country as well as extensive fauna; from the highly endangered Arabian leopards in the Hajar Mountains to gerbils and geckos. The animals you are most likely to see though, are camels and goats (often roaming dangerously close to the roadside).

The birdlife is reasonably extensive but the most impressive array of natural life is to be found beneath the waves. A myriad of tropical fish, as well as dolphins, turtles, small sharks, and the elusive dugong, are just some of the marine creatures you may spot along Abu Dhabi's 600km of coastline. For more information on diving or snorkelling refer to page 116.

This map is not an authority on international boundaries

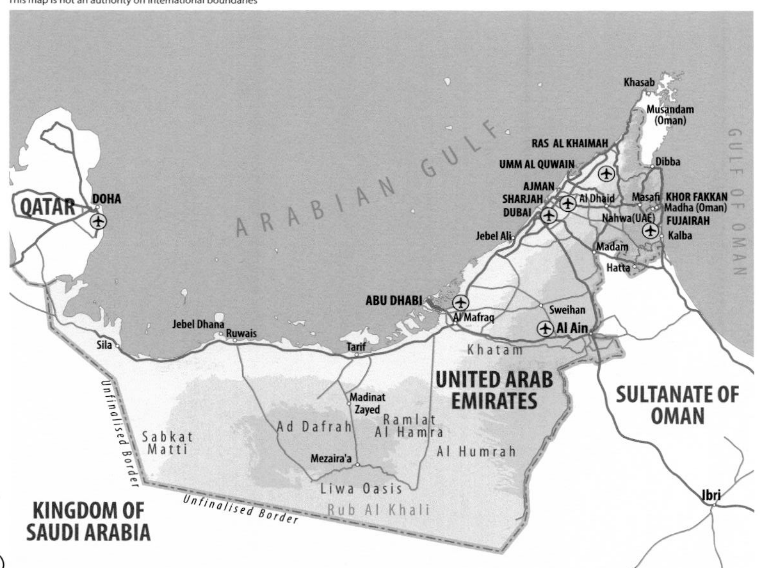

History

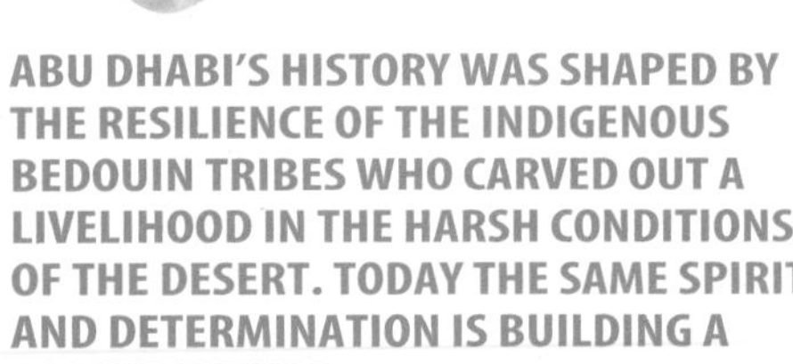

ABU DHABI'S HISTORY WAS SHAPED BY THE RESILIENCE OF THE INDIGENOUS BEDOUIN TRIBES WHO CARVED OUT A LIVELIHOOD IN THE HARSH CONDITIONS OF THE DESERT. TODAY THE SAME SPIRIT AND DETERMINATION IS BUILDING A BRIGHT FUTURE.

It is hard to reconcile the modern city of Abu Dhabi with the scattered settlement of arish (palm frond) huts that existed in the 1950s. Documentation of Abu Dhabi's history is scarce but the emirate is rich in archaeological finds. Evidence of settlements have been found around Marawah, Dalma, Jebel Hafeet near Al Ain, and on the island of Umm al Nar near Abu Dhabi city, some dating to more than 7,000 years ago. Abu Dhabi's history really begins with the Bani Yas Bedouin tribe who are known to have been in the area along the coast by the 16th century.

In 1761, following the discovery of fresh water, the leader of the Bani Yas tribe moved his people to the island. The island was comparatively fertile and the abundance of wildlife led to its name (Abu Dhabi, translated, means 'land of the gazelle'). This initial settlement was soon followed by the relocation of the ruling Al Nahyan family from the Liwa Oasis in the south of the country. By the 1800s the town had developed considerably through the trade and sale of pearls. From 1855 to 1909, under the reign of Sheikh Zayed bin Khalifa (also known as 'Zayed the Great'), Abu Dhabi prospered. It was during his rule, in 1892, that Abu Dhabi and the emirates to the north agreed

An Admired Ruler

The late Sheikh Zayed bin Sultan Al Nahyan was revered by his peers and adored by the public. As UAE president for 33 years and Ruler of Abu Dhabi from 1966, he was responsible for many major economic and social advances both in Abu Dhabi and throughout the country, and his vision laid the foundations for today's modern society.

to let Britain handle, exclusively, its international relations, building on a series of treaties that dated back to 1820. The area was seen as an important link with India and the east and became known as the Trucial States (or Trucial Coast).

Abu Dhabi's fortunes faltered following the death of Zayed the Great, when the combination of world recession and the creation of the cultured pearl industry in Japan impacted Abu Dhabi's wealth.

In 1939, Sheikh Shakhbut bin Sultan Al Nahyan granted a concession to an international consortium to search for oil onshore. The huge offshore reserves were not discovered until 1958 (there was an onshore find a year later). Exports began four years later, launching Abu Dhabi on its way to incredible wealth. In 1966, the ruling family decided that Sheikh Zayed, then ruler's representative in Al Ain, should replace his brother, Sheikh Shakhbut, as ruler.

In 1968, the British announced that they would withdraw from the region by the end of 1971, and the ruling sheikhs realised that by joining forces they would have a stronger regional and global voice. And so, the federation of the United Arab Emirates was created. Sheikh Zayed was elected as the first president – a position he held until his death in 2004. Under the federation the emirates all maintained a certain degree of autonomy and the revenue generated by Abu Dhabi's massive oil reserves allowed Sheikh Zayed to undertake a far-reaching programme of development within his own emirate. He was much loved and is acknowledged as the 'Father of the Nation'.

Following Sheikh Zayed's death in 2004, his son, Sheikh Khalifa bin Zayed Al Nahyan, was elected as the new president of the UAE. Sheikh Khalifa, who has been involved in government

for nearly 40 years, has promised to preserve his father's legacy and ensure continued growth. Apart from being an oil expert and head of the Supreme Petroleum Council, Sheikh Khalifa is renowned for his love of traditional sports, and his efforts in preserving them in today's times.

His first years as president have been marked by some exciting developments, including Al Gurm Resort, Saadiyat Island and The Central Market.

From its small beginnings as a pearling settlement, Abu Dhabi has come a long way in the last 50 years. Its population has grown from just 15,000 in 1962 to closer to 1.8 million today. Oil revenues have been invested wisely to create an impressive modern society and first-class infrastructure. Tourism is a key priority in the government's ambitious diversification plans, with a target of 3 million visitors by 2015.

Abu Dhabi Timeline

1760 The Baniyas Tribe finds fresh water on the island of Abu Dhabi and decides to settle there.

1795 The Old Fort is built (also known as Qasr Al Hosn or the White Fort).

1820 First treaty between Abu Dhabi and Britain.

1835 Maritime Truce signed between the Trucial States and Britain.

1892 Exclusive agreement with Britain.

1958 First oil is discovered offshore.

1961 Abu Dhabi's first paved road is constructed.

1962 Abu Dhabi begins exporting oil.

1966 Sheikh Zayed bin Sultan Al Nahyan becomes ruler of Abu Dhabi.

1971 Britain withdraws from the Gulf. The United Arab Emirates is born, with HH Sheikh Zayed bin Sultan Al Nahyan as the leader. The UAE joins the Arab League.

1973 The UAE launches a single currency, the UAE dirham.

1981 The GCC is formed, with the UAE as a founding member.

2003 Etihad, the UAE's official airline, is launched.

2004 Sheikh Zayed bin Sultan Al Nahyan dies and is succeeded as President of the UAE and Ruler of Abu Dhabi by his son, Sheikh Khalifa bin Zayed Al Nahyan.

2004 Abu Dhabi Tourism Authority created.

Abu Dhabi Tomorrow

ABU DHABI IS A CITY THAT DREAMS BIG. THE FUTURE PROMISES TO BE NOTHING SHORT SPECTACULAR. THE ISLAND'S COASTLINE IS TO HOST SPARKLING NEW DEVELOPMENTS, BRINGING MUSEUMS OF INTERNATIONAL RENOWN AND A RANGE OF INNOVATIVE LUXURY HOTEL PROPERTIES.

Abu Dhabi has entered a new era of dramatic development that will over the next 10 years will propel the emirate into one of the world's leading centres of excellence in tourism, culture, infrastructure development and across a wide spectrum of business and social activity. The physical transformation will be truly spectacular. A series of massive investment projects promise to establish Abu Dhabi as one of the architectural wonders of the world. The hallmarks of these developments will be innovation, harmony, quality and style. Most of them will be outside the city centre thus ensuring that construction for the future does not spoil enjoyment of the present.

Abu Dhabi International Airport www.abudhabiairport.ae
Abu Dhabi International Airport's current US$6.8 billion expansion and redevelopment plan involves the construction of a new midfield passenger terminal, cargo and maintenance facilities and other commercial developments. The project will provide a top-quality home base for Etihad, the national airline of the UAE, and facilitate the expansion of its operations. The

new facilities will have an initial handling capacity of 20 million passengers a year when they open in 2010, ultimately rising to 50 million annually.

Abu Dhabi National Exhibition Centre www.adnec.ae

With the first phase completed in February 2007, the new Abu Dhabi National Exhibition Centre complex will eventually include 57,000 square metres of gross exhibition floor space, a massive

21,000 square metres of visitor concourse and 7,500 square metres of multi-purpose halls. The complex will also feature dedicated conference facilities for 1,200 people, banqueting areas and more than 30 high-specification meeting rooms. It will form the heart of Capital Centre, a major new mixed use tourism, commercial and residential development.

Al Gurm Resort & Spa

www.algurmresort.com

The Al Gurm Resort & Spa is under construction among the mangroves off the Coast Road, on the west of the island, and will be an eco-friendly development. The 161 suite luxury hotel is scheduled to open in late 2007, with luxury villas and signature island villas opening at a later date. In total there will be 59 homes, situated along a private beach.

Al Raha

Already well known for its lovely beach, the Al Raha district close to the airport is to be transformed through the development of a 6.8 million square metre site. It will reach along the highway on reclaimed land and offer residential, cultural and entertainment facilities as well as several new hotels.

Al Reem Island

A major residential, commercial and business project is to be built on the natural island of Al Reem, located just 300 metres off the north-eastern coast of Abu Dhabi city. The island will eventually accommodate 280,000 inhabitants and a range of amenities like schools, shopping malls, restaurants, a 27-hole golf course, hotels, resorts, spas, gardens and beaches. Shams

Abu Dhabi is one of the three projects being built on Al Reem. This $6.9 billion project will contain around 100 skyscrapers (including the 83 storey Sky Tower), 22,000 residential units and a million square metre park. Another is the $8 billion Najmat Abu Dhabi, a world class, integrated, multi-functional and mixed use project. Property on Al Reem is available to all nationalities on an extendable 99 year leasehold basis.

The Central Market

www.aldar.com

This market promises to become a major landmark in the heart of the city. The project is transforming Abu Dhabi's central souk area, on Hamdan Street, into a modern development with apartments, an Arabian-style souk, restaurants, office space and a mosque. The first phase is expected to be completed by summer 2008.

Corniche Redevelopment

Abu Dhabi's showpiece seafront esplanade, the corniche, has undergone massive redevelopment over the last few years. This work has included the creation of a number of attractive public parks, walkways and cycle paths.

Emirates Pearl

The Emirates Pearl will be a sparkly addition to Abu Dhabi's soaring skyline. The 47 storey block has been designed by Aussie architect Dennis Lems and will sit on a 22 metre high podium, housing restaurants and shops. The tower itself will hold a hotel and apartments.

Khalidiya Mall

www.emkegroup.com

Construction is now complete on the much-anticipated Khalidiya Mall, which spreads across 80,000 square metres over two floors. The mall is designed in distinctive Islamic architectural style, and includes an atrium, a summer garden, fountains, cafes and a foodcourt.

The Quay Development

The city's Tourist Club area is to be redeveloped on quite a grand scale. There will be a stack of new leisure, residential and commercial buildings, including a 620 room, five-star hotel, shops and office blocks. It will have Abu Dhabi's first aquarium, a gated residential community of around 400 apartments available to lease and office space. The whole development will be known simply as 'The Quay' and will include a 60 berth marina. There will also be a public promenade for visitors to stroll along and a range of harbour-view cafes and restaurants. Construction of The Quay should be completed by 2010.

Saadiyat Island

www.saadiyat.ae

Located on a 27 square kilometre natural island 500 metres off the coast of Abu Dhabi city is a huge residential, business, cultural and leisure development. It will incorporate two championship golf courses, 19km of beaches and a range of top class leisure, entertainment and cultural facilities including the Guggenheim and Louvre museums. A staggering 29 hotels have been planned as well as 8,000 villas and 38,000 apartments. To be developed in three phases the entire project should be completed by 2018.

Shams Abu Dhabi

www.sorouh.com

Shams Abu Dhabi is a self-contained community being built on Al Reem island close to Abu Dhabi. Bisected by canals and pedestrian walkways, it will include commercial, entertainment and residential districts, as well as a five-star hotel and a marina. Completion is due in 2011.

Yas Island (featuring Ferrari World)

The 2,500 hectares of Yas Island will feature attractions such as Ferrari World, a branded theme park set to open in 2009. It will have a Grand Prix circuit and attractions for all the family. Yas Island will also have hotels, a water park, a 300,000 square metre retail area, golf courses, marinas, polo clubs, apartments, villas and numerous food and beverage outlets.

Doing Business in Abu Dhabi

IF YOU'VE SPOTTED A BUSINESS OPPORTUNITY DURING YOUR STAY IN ABU DHABI THERE IS PLENTY OF SUPPORT AVAILABLE – NOT LEAST NEW ECONOMIC ZONES WHICH ALLOW COMPLETE FOREIGN OWNERSHIP OF COMPANIES.

Abu Dhabi is unique. You have all the conveniences of 'big city' life, but without the need for long commutes, traffic jams and crowded public transport. People work hard, but there is a far greater balance between work and home life than in many other cities around the world. Families do far more together and make the most of the many parks and beaches to relax and enjoy themselves, particularly during the cooler winter months.

Investing in Abu Dhabi

Private and overseas investment is actively encouraged in Abu Dhabi, with the emirate now allowing 100% foreign ownership of businesses in various designated economic zones, such as the Industrial City of Abu Dhabi (ICAD). Export of non oil related products has tripled since 1990 and continues to rise. In addition to various government departments that are specifically responsible for providing commercial assistance to enterprises in Abu Dhabi, there are various chambers of commerce and other business groups that help facilitate investments and provide opportunities for networking with others in the community. Some groups provide information on trade with their respective country, as well as on business opportunities both in Abu Dhabi and the other emirates. Most also arrange social and networking events. Refer to the Abu Dhabi Yellow Pages and Hawk Business Pages for details. Both directories are available online (www.yellow pages.net.ae, www.hawk pages.com). Another useful website is The Emirates Network (www.theemiratesnetwork.com) – an online facility that allows you to access the specialised business directories in the UAE.

Culture

ABU DHABI'S ARCHITECTURE MAY BE MODERN AND INTERNATIONAL BUT ITS CULTURE IS FIRMLY ROOTED IN THE ISLAMIC TRADITIONS OF ARABIA. THIS IS THE EPITOME OF MIDDLE EAST MEETS MODERN WEST.

The UAE's culture is tolerant and welcoming, and visitors are sure to be charmed by the genuine friendliness of the people. Abu Dhabi is a melting pot of nationalities and cultures, all of which are embraced without losing the cultural and national identity of which the UAE's people are justifiably proud; a culture and heritage inextricably linked to its religion. Women face no discrimination and are able to drive and walk around the city unescorted.

The rapid economic development of the last 40 years has, in many ways, changed life in the UAE beyond recognition. However, despite rapid development and increased exposure to foreign influences, indigenous traditions and culture are alive and thriving. The people of Abu Dhabi enthusiastically promote cultural and sporting events that are representative of their past, such as falconry, camel racing and traditional dhow sailing. At times it may seem like the national sport is shopping, but many important traditions are retained. Arabic poetry, dances, songs and traditional art are encouraged, and weddings and celebrations are still colourful occasions of feasting and music. As a mark of pride in the culture and national identity, most locals wear traditional national dress. For men this is a dishdash(a) – a full length shirt-dress that is worn with a white or red checked

Call to Prayer

There are five calls to prayer each day. They are Fajr at dawn, Thuher in the middle of the day, Asr at mid-afternoon, Maghrib at sunset, and Isha at nightfall. Mosques around Abu Dhabi are adorned with loud speakers, meaning you'll never miss the distinctive and atmospheric call to prayer.

head-dress (gutra) which is held in place with a black cord (agal). Women wear a black abaya – a long, loose black robe, and a sheyla – a headscarf. Some women also wear a thin black veil to cover their faces and older women sometimes wear a leather mask (burkha).

Religion & Ramadan

Islam is the official religion in the UAE and is widely practised. The religion is based on five pillars (Faith, Prayer, Charity, Fasting and Pilgrimage) and Muslims are called upon to pray five times a day, with these times varying according to the position of the sun. It is worth keeping in mind that Islam is more than just a religion, it is the basis for a complete way of life that all Muslims adhere to. There are plenty of mosques dotted around the city and, while most people pray in them when possible, most offices and public buildings have rooms set aside for prayers. Also it's not unusual to see people kneeling by the side of the road if they are not near a mosque. It is considered impolite to stare at people praying or to walk over prayer mats. The abundance of mosques does of course mean that the call to prayer can be heard five times a day from the loudspeakers of the many different minarets, and not always in sync! Friday is the Islamic holy day and pretty much everything will be closed until mid-afternoon, in accordance with the state and Islamic law.

During the holy month of Ramadan, Muslims are obliged to fast during daylight hours. Non-Muslims are expected to do likewise out of respect, and you should not eat, drink or smoke in public areas during the fasting hours. You should also dress more conservatively. At sunset, the fast is broken with the Iftar feast. All over the city, festive Ramadan tents are filled each evening with people of all nationalities and religions enjoying shisha and traditional Arabic mezze and sweets. In addition to the standard shisha cafes and restaurants around town, many hotels erect special Ramadan tents for the month.

The timing of Ramadan is not fixed in terms of the western calendar, but each year it occurs approximately 11 days earlier than the previous year, with the start date depending on the sighting of the moon. In 2007, Ramadan began on 13 September so it should be declared around 1 September

2008. Parks and shops open and close later (many are closed during the day), entertainment such as live music is stopped, and cinemas limit daytime screenings. Eid Al Fitr (Feast of The Breaking of the Fast) is a three-day celebration and holiday at the end of Ramadan, when the new moon is spotted. It is the year's main religious event, like Diwali for Hindus and Christmas for Christians.

Local Cuisine

Abu Dhabi's restaurant scene has a truly global flavour, with most of the world's major national cuisines represented, and many of the fast-food outlets too. Eating out is very popular, but people tend to go out late so restaurants are often quiet in the early evenings. Modern Arabic cuisine reflects a blend of Moroccan, Tunisian, Iranian and Egyptian cooking styles, but the term usually refers to Lebanese food. From pavement stands serving mouth-watering shawarma (lamb or chicken sliced from a spit) and falafel (mashed and fried chickpea balls) sandwiches to the more elaborate khouzi (whole roast lamb served on a bed of rice, mixed with nuts), it's all here and it's all delicious.

National Flag

The UAE flag has three equal horizontal bands: green at the top, white in the middle and black at the bottom, with a thicker, vertical band of red running down the hoist side. The colours on the flag are common to many Arab nations and they symbolise Arab unity and independence.

Arabic Coffee

Traditional Arabic coffee is served on many occasions

Overview

and, if offered, it is gracious to accept because coffee plays a special role as a symbolic expression of welcome. Even the pot itself, with its characteristic shape and long spout, has come to depict Arab hospitality. Freshly ground and flavoured with cardamom, Arabic coffee comes in tiny cups with no handles. The cup should be taken with the right hand. The server will stand by with the pot and fill the cups when empty. It's normal to take one or two then signal you have had enough by shaking the cup gently from side to side. Until you shake the cup, the server will continue topping it up!

Pork

Pork is not part of the Arabic menu and the consumption of it is taboo to a Muslim. Many restaurants don't serve it, though

you should find it on the menu in some of the larger hotels and it is also available in some supermarkets such as Abela and Spinneys.

Alcohol

Alcohol is served in licensed outlets associated with hotels and a few clubs (such as golf clubs). Restaurants which are not part of hotels are not allowed to serve alcohol. Non muslim residents can, however, obtain a licence to purchase alcohol for consumption at home.

Social & Business Hours

The working week begins on Sunday, with Friday and Saturday being considered the weekend. Friday is the holy day. While private offices tend to work similar hours to those in the west, with 09:00 until 18:00 considered normal, government departments will start and finish earlier. The opening times for embassies and consulates vary but are usually from 08:00 to 14:30, Sunday to Thursday.

Most shops operate split shifts, though the outlets in many of the big shopping malls open at 10:00 and close between 22:00 and 24:00. Some food shops and petrol stations are open 24 hours a day. Most shops don't open until around 15:00 on Fridays, though corner shops only close during prayer times, and will stay open till 22:00.

During the holy month of Ramadan food outlets and restaurants generally remain closed during the day, opening for Iftar, though some provide takeaway services during the day. Shops also tend to stay open later, some until midnight.

Exploring

A Land of Contrasts

ABU DHABI OFFERS A MULTITUDE OF ACTIVITIES, SIGHTS AND EXCITEMENTS FOR VISITORS. YOU CAN ENJOY THE OUTSTANDING LUXURY AND FASCINATING HERITAGE OF A BUSTLING ISLAND CITY, BUT WITHOUT THE CROWDS.

Between the calm green gardens, high-rise apartment blocks, elegant fountains, stunning corniche and luxury villas, is a truly vibrant city. Abu Dhabi is growing rapidly, and its evolution from quiet village to thriving metropolis has been remarkable, a testament to the vision of the late Sheikh Zayed, and the energy and drive of its people.

The high-rise central business district is home to imaginatively designed buildings which provide a dramatic backdrop to the corniche area. The corniche itself is designed for play, with beautiful parks, walkways, cycle paths and picnic areas, all bordering the turquoise waters of the Arabian Gulf. Further inland the high-rises make way for beautiful villas, low-rise apartment blocks and quieter, tree-lined streets.

The following section gives an idea of what there is to see and do in Abu Dhabi – interesting places to visit, including museums, heritage sites, parks and beaches. If you're short of time, an organised tour (p.92) is a great way to make the most of your visit. There's also a brief overview of what the other emirates have to offer. For more information, check out the ***Abu Dhabi Explorer***.

Visitors' Checklist

Abu Dhabi Corniche p.50
The ultimate place for an evening stroll, the recently redeveloped corniche is a great place to pause and gaze out to sea.

Al Ain Museum p.83
Housed in an old fort, the museum houses a display of photos from the days before the oil boom, Bedouin jewellery, weapons and a reconstruction of a traditional majlis.

Al Ain Oasis p.83
This shaded, tranquil oasis contains many plantations, some of which are still working farms with ancient falaj irrigation systems.

Corniche Cruises p.91
For the best views that Abu Dhabi has to offer, from a unique vantage point, a cruise along the corniche cannot be beaten – don't forget your camera.

Culture Buffs p.61
The Cultural Foundation holds displays of Islamic and international art, music recitals and theatre productions throughout the year. The Old Fort in the same compound dates back to 1793.

Desert Delights p.94
Take an organised tour to experience the vast Arabian desert in style and comfort. After a thrilling rollercoaster drive over the dunes you'll enjoy a sumptuous barbecue under the stars at a Bedouin camp.

Dhow Building p.52
The craftsmen in the dhow yards at Al Bateen use traditional tools and techniques to build the majestic craft seen racing off the corniche, and the cargo dhows used in the Gulf and Indian Ocean.

Henna
Traditional henna designs on your hands or feet are a great souvenir of your visit. The art is offered by most salons and if you don't like it, you can wash it off after a couple of weeks.

Gold Souk p.136

The Gold Souk in Madinat Zayed is a great place to pick up a bargain. A vast range of regional and international jewellery is available.

Heritage Village p.46

The Heritage Village is a must-see for all visitors. It offers a glimpse into pre-oil life in Abu Dhabi, where you can try out the effectiveness of windtower air conditioning or get up close with a camel.

Hili Archaeological Garden p.84

A Bronze Age settlement, thought to be over 4,000 years old. Children will enjoy the gardens and play area. Fossil Valley is nearby.

Iranian Souk p.147

The eclectic range of goods on sale at Abu Dhabi's Iranian Souk make for an impressive sight. It is near the fish market and stock arrives by boat from Iran twice a week.

Island Expedition p.91

The islands around the capital are great places to explore and organised trips can take you out for a day to enjoy the peace and seclusion. Futaisi Island is great for wildlife.

Liwa p.94

With some of the world's biggest sand dunes and unforgettable sun rises, the long trip out to Liwa shouldn't be missed. There's good off-road driving to be had in the area too.

Shop Till You Drop p.128

Shopping in Abu Dhabi is hard to beat, whether you're looking for the latest designer labels or souvenirs. The city has an impressive range of shops, but doesn't yet suffer from overcrowding.

Shisha p.152

The scent of shisha tobacco is evocative of this region. The best shisha places in town are the cafes on the Breakwater where you can sit and enjoy the panoramic city views.

Ras Al Akhdar & Breakwater

LOCATED IN THE NORTH-WESTERN CORNER OF THE ISLAND, RAS AL AKHDAR'S PRIDE IS THE ICONIC EMIRATES PALACE HOTEL AND FINE PUBLIC BEACHES. THE NEARBY BREAKWATER IS HOME TO ABU DHABI'S LARGEST MALL, THE HERITAGE VILLAGE AND SOME OF THE CITY'S MOST IMPRESSIVE VIEWS.

Ras Al Akhdar is the area at the north-western tip of Abu Dhabi island. It is dominated by the Emirates Palace Hotel (p.221), reputedly the most expensive hotel ever built. This is definitely not somewhere for the budget traveller as it has been designed to epitomise luxury. The classical architecture is complemented by state-of-the-art technology and the hotel houses a number of the capital's top restaurants (see Going Out p.148). The area's other attractions include the Abu Dhabi Ladies Club which houses the luxurious Le Spa. This members club for ladies only has excellent leisure facilities – non-members are welcome to attend exercise classes and the spa. You'll also find privacy and excellent facilities on the Ladies' Beach, making this the ideal leisure spot for women in the capital.

Top Scores
What's your flavour?

Culture	●●●●
Shopping	●●●●●
Sun	●●
Luxury	●●●●
Budget	●●●
Kids	●●●●

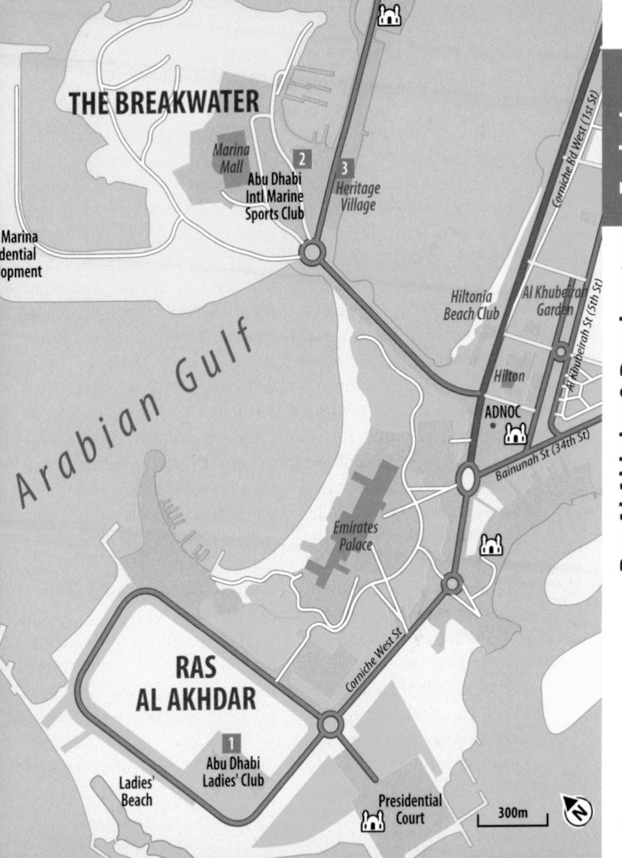
THE BREAKWATER
Marina Mall
2
Abu Dhabi Intl Marine Sports Club
3
Heritage Village
Marina
idential
elopment
Corniche Rd West (1st St)
Hiltonia Beach Club
Al Khubeirah Garden
Al Khubeirah St (5th St)
Hilton
ADNOC
Bainunah St (34th St)
Arabian Gulf
Emirates Palace
Corniche West St
RAS AL AKHDAR
1
Abu Dhabi Ladies' Club
Ladies' Beach
Presidential Court
300m
N

As well as the beach, it has a cafeteria and a pool. There are also several open beaches in the area, which are quiet during the week but get very busy at weekends.

The Breakwater is an area of reclaimed land connected by a causeway to the corniche. The beachfront walkways are an extension of the corniche development, and offer some spectacular views of the city. Marina Mall (p.136), is the capital's largest mall, and is packed with a host of international brands, a multi-screen cinema and many other leisure facilities. Phase two is the destination of choice for the city's label-conscious fashionistas. Phase three has recently opened and the complex has a 100m viewing tower and SnowWorld, an indoor snow and ice fantasy land where you can go ice-skating or skiing; even when it's sizzling outside. It's a wonderful spot to escape the intense summer heat and practice your turns.

The Abu Dhabi International Marine Sports Club hosts numerous international and local powerboating events – the calm waters between the corniche, Breakwater and

Breakwater Boom

Development of the Breakwater is ongoing. The latest phase, the construction of the new marina and luxury housing development behind Marina Mall, was recently completed, with villas already occupied by tenants. One of the most famous landmarks on the Breakwater is the enormous flagpole next to the Heritage Village. For some time this was the tallest unsupported flagpole in the world (123m), until Jordan erected an even taller one (126m) in 2003.

Lulu Island are perfect for smaller powerboats. The club has a marina, workshops and a showroom stocking marine sports and fishing accessories.

The fascinating Heritage Village overlooks the corniche. It is run by the Emirates Heritage Club and gives an interesting insight into the way that life used to be. The displays in this attractive open air museum set out to illustrate traditional aspects of Bedouin life, including a campfire with coffee pots, a goat-hair tent, a well and an ancient irrigation system (falaj).

You can test the effectiveness of the earliest form of air conditioning by standing under the windtower in the traditional houses made of barasti (dried palm leaves). There are loads of great photo opportunities, such as the chance to get up close and personal with an Arabian horse or a camel.

Workshops on traditional skills such as metal work, pottery and weaving are given by local craftsmen who are happy to share their skills – they are friendly and informative and may even let you have a go yourself.

You can pick up local craft items in the shop, and the spice shop is stocked full of dried herbs, handmade soap, and exotic spices (you can buy saffron, the world's most expensive spice, at excellent prices).

Once you've wandered around outside, head into the air-conditioned museum which houses a collection of artefacts including coffee pots, diving tools, Holy Qurans, jewellery, weapons and garments.

After visiting the village, sample some typical Arabic cuisine at the beachside restaurant. It has a great view of the corniche, and it's close to a pleasant kids' play area.

1 Abu Dhabi Ladies Club

Al Ras Al Akhdar www.abudhabiladiesclub.com 02 666 2228

This excellent leisure facility has a gym, pool and fitness studio, as well as a library, computers, arts and crafts classes, and the luxurious Le Spa. Although originally a members-only club, non-members can now buy a day pass for under Dhs.100, or short-term memberships (two weeks or one month). These allow full use of the club's facilities.

2 Abu Dhabi International Marine Sports Club

Breakwater www.adimsc.ae 02 681 5566

The Abu Dhabi International Marine Sports Club is the organising body for local and international powerboat events, traditional watersports and jetski races. The club has a marina with serviced berths, workshops and a showroom which stocks marine sports and fishing accessories.

3 Heritage Village

Breakwater 02 681 4455

The Heritage Village offers an interesting glimpse into the country's past. It is the best way to get a feel of what life was like in Abu Dhabi years ago, long before the discovery of oil and the subsequent development. Learn more about traditional crafts directly from local craftsmen who are happy to show you how it's done. It is a fantastic place to shop for souvenirs, like authentic pottery or exotic spices. It is open daily from 09:00 until 13:00 and from 17:00 until 21:00 except Fridays when the hours are 16:00 to 21:00.

ARABIAN OUD

Ras Al Akhdar & Breakwater

In the Area For...

One Hour

Head straight for the opulence of **Emirates Palace**, where you can experience unimaginable levels of luxury. Treat yourself to traditional afternoon tea in Le Café.

Half Day

The **Heritage Village** is the closest you'll get to travelling back in time with its displays of Bedouin life. Then catapult yourself back into the future with a whirlwind visit to the nearby **Marina Mall**, which has over 250 shops and a 110m high viewing tower – the ultimate photo opportunity.

Full Day

Wander around the **Heritage Village** at leisure and observe local men and women sharing their skills in traditional crafts. Enjoy a lunch break in one of the many food outlets inside the **Marina Mall,** followed by a shopping spree in the multitude of retail outlets stocking the world's most luxurious brands. You'll soon be able to chill out in Snow World or head for the top of the 100m viewing tower for a dramatic sunset view. For dinner, stay local and enjoy some authentic Arabic cuisine at one of the restaurants overlooking the corniche.

Corniche West

WITH TWO OF THE CITY'S TOP HOTELS, A NUMBER OF BEAUTIFUL PARKS, GREAT VIEWS AND AN AIR OF TRANQUILITY, THIS IS ONE OF THE CAPITAL'S MOST AFFLUENT AREAS.

In the west of the city, the corniche begins at the end of the causeway to the Breakwater. The Hilton Abu Dhabi (p.222) stands on the land side while the Hiltonia Beach Club has pride of place on the sea side. The Hilton is one of the city's older hotels but is still one of its most luxurious. The bars and restaurants that it houses are always busy so if you are hoping to head here for an evening out it's best to book ahead. The Hiltonia Beach Club was remodelled during the redevelopment of the corniche and is one of Abu Dhabi's most popular beach clubs, especially at the weekends. This was one of the first stretches of the corniche to be completed and its parks and green areas are popular for picnics and get-togethers.

Al Bateen is home to the InterContinental Abu Dhabi, another of the city's well-established luxury hotels, which was completely renovated and refurbished in 2006.

Further along the coast is the Bateen jetty (there are a number

Top Scores
What's your flavour?

Culture	●●●
Shopping	●●●
Sun	●●●●
Luxury	●●●●
Budget	●●
Kids	●●●

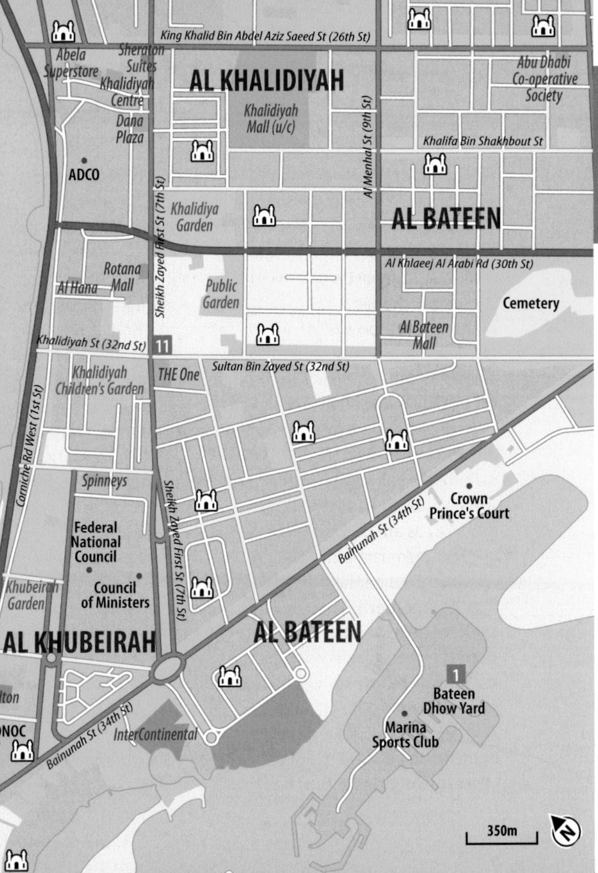
King Khalid Bin Abdel Aziz Saeed St (26th St)
Abela Superstore
Sheraton Suites
Khalidiyah Centre
Dana Plaza
AL KHALIDIYAH
Khalidiyah Mall (u/c)
Abu Dhabi Co-operative Society
Al Menhal St (9th St)
Khalifa Bin Shakhbout St
ADCO
Sheikh Zayed First St (7th St)
Khalidiya Garden
AL BATEEN
Al Khlaeej Al Arabi Rd (30th St)
Rotana Mall
Al Hana
Public Garden
Cemetery
Al Bateen Mall
Khalidiyah St (32nd St)
11
Sultan Bin Zayed St (32nd St)
Khalidiyah Children's Garden
THE One
Corniche Rd West (1st St)
Spinneys
Sheikh Zayed First St (7th St)
Crown Prince's Court
Bainunah St (34th St)
Federal National Council
Council of Ministers
Khubeirah Garden
AL KHUBEIRAH
AL BATEEN
1
Bateen Dhow Yard
Hilton
ADNOC
Bainunah St (34th St)
InterContinental
Marina Sports Club
350m
N

of marine supply stores around it) and the Bateen dhow yard. A visit to the dhow yard is essential, not just to absorb the evocative smells of freshly cut African and Indian teak, but also to watch craftsmen build magnificent dhows and racing vessels using age-old techniques. These wooden vessels can still be seen during dhow races off the corniche or plying the trade routes around the Gulf and across the Indian Ocean.

This is a sought-after residential area in Abu Dhabi, with a mix of low-rise apartment blocks and villas, along with great parks and a number of coffee shops. The Khalidiya Public Garden, which was recently revamped, and the Khalidiya Children's Garden (ladies and children only), are both popular for evening visits and weekend picnics.

Two of the city's largest supermarkets, Spinneys and Abela, are also in this area of town. They stock a lot of imported items so if there's something that you are missing from home, make them your first port of call.

1 Bateen Dhow Yard

Al Bateen

The skilled craftsmen in this fascinating boat yard use traditional techniques to construct the dhows, which are still used for racing and for trade throughout the Gulf region and the Indian Ocean. Visit in the early evening and not only will you be able to get some wonderful photos of the sun setting behind the hulls, but you may also be able to talk to the craftsmen – if they are not too busy they are usually happy to share an insight into their traditional craft.

Hilton

Corniche West

In the Area For...

One Hour

Enjoy a bit of downtime at the great cafe inside **THE One** furniture shop. Not only is the decor amazing, but the menu is innovative – apart from the delicious cakes and pastries, it also includes imaginative treats like parmesan ice-cream.

Half Day

Head out to the **Breakwater** to browse around the outlets at **Marina Mall,** then get a taste of pre-oil Abu Dhabi at the **Heritage Village.** Hop in a taxi and head to the **Al Bateen dhow yard** at around sunset (the best time for photos and chatting to the craftsmen).

Full Day

With the **Heritage Village** so close by, you can spend the morning wandering around it, learning about life before air conditioning, oil and major developments. Stop for a late lunch in **Marina Mall** before heading out to the major highlight of the area: the **Al Bateen dhow yard.** Aim to get there before sunset to have a wander round, and then get your camera out as the sun goes down to get some amazing shots of the imposing hulls of the dhows in front of the sunset. This is also a good time to chat to the craftsmen to find out more about their age-old techniques and basic tools. Round off the day with a traditional meal at one of the Arabic restaurants on the Breakwater.

Corniche East & Central Abu Dhabi

WITH THE GREEN AND TRANQUIL CORNICHE RUNNING ALONGSIDE THE CLEAR BLUE WATERS OF THE GULF, AND THE ADJACENT HIGH-RISE HUSTLE AND BUSTLE OF ABU DHABI CITY, THIS IS AN AREA OF CONTRASTS.

The redevelopment of Abu Dhabi's iconic corniche involved the reclaiming of a large strip of land and the creation of a number of new parks and attractions. The high-rise buildings which overlook it were once only separated from the sea by a six-lane road, but now a lush strip of greenery sits on the other side. An evening stroll along the corniche should be part of every visit to the capital – this is where many of the city's residents come to meet, have picnics and relax, especially in the evenings and at weekends.

This area is generally seen as the city centre or main business district. Among the high-rises is the oldest building in the capital, the 'Qasr Al Hosn' (the Old Fort, also known as the White Fort or Fort Palace), which dates back to 1793. It was the official residence of the rulers of Abu Dhabi for many years. While the fort itself is not open to the public, within its grounds

Top Scores
What's your flavour?

Culture	•••
Shopping	•••••
Sun	•••
Luxury	•••
Budget	••••
Kids	•••

Corniche Hospital
Al Diar Mina
Al Diar Regency
Sheraton
International Rotana Inn
Al Diar Dana
Electra St
TOURIST CLUB AREA
As Salam St (8th St)
Al Falah St (9th St)
Lulu Centre
Hamdan Bin Mohamed St (5th St)
Sheikh Zayed First St (7th St)
9th St
Al Ain Palace
Le Royal Meridien
Diplomatic
Zakher
Millennium
Grand Continental
Dr. McCulloch's Clinic
Corniche Rd East
Khalifa Bin Zayed St (3rd St)
Crowne Plaza
Bhs
Al Diar Sands
Bani Yas St (6th St)
Lulu St (4th St)
Hamdan Centre
Corniche Residence Hilton
Al Noor Hospital
Novotel Centre
Al Sharqi St (4th St)
AL DHAFRAH
L MARKAZIYAH
New Souk
Liwa Centre
Liwa St
Madinat Zayed
Gold Souk
Central Post Office
Al Falah Plaza
Petroleum Exhibition
Central Market (u/c)
MADINAT ZAYED
Al Diar Palm
Fotouh Al Khair
New Medical Centre
Etisalat
Chamber Commerce
Fish Market & Vegetable Souk
2
1
Cultural Foundation
Sheikh Rashid Bin Saeed Al Maktoum St (2nd St)
Qasr Al Hosn
Khalid Bin Waleed St (22nd St)
Al Muhairy Centre
Grand Stores
Central Hospital
Corniche Rd West
Bainunah Hilton Tower
Tariq Bin Zayed St
Al Manhal Palace
Al Manhal St (9th St)
Sheikh Khalifa Medical City
AL HOSN
AL MANHAL
AL ZAAB
Sheikh Zayed First St (7th St)
Al Markaziyah Garden
Al Hosn Plaza
Agriculture Research Laboratory
350m
N

sits the Cultural Foundation, home to the National Library and the Institution of Culture and Art. Each year it holds a number of art exhibitions, classical music recitals and film screenings.

Sheikh Hamdan bin Mohammed Street (known as Hamdan Street) is a haven for avid shoppers, with local and international stores sharing the limelight with a number of independent restaurants and entertainment venues.

At the end of Hamdan Street is the Marks & Spencer mall (Fotouh Al Khair Centre, p.138), which houses a number of international stores and a great cafe.

Further up Hamdan Street is the site of the old Central Souk. The area is currently under redevelopment but there is a small area of the souk that remains, just off Khalifa bin Zayed Street. Gold is an excellent purchase while you are in this region, and you'll find plenty of it in one of the many jewellery shops lining the street before the Liwa Centre (p.139). So much gold is packed into the windows of these shops that at night the dazzling yellow glow spills out onto the pavements. The Hamdan Centre (p.138) is something of an institution and should be a stop on every

Intrepid Explorers

While we like to think that we have covered every inch of Abu Dhabi, filtered out the missable and highlighted the unmissable, you may feel differently. So if you think we've left something out then we would love to hear your suggestions. Maybe it's an undiscovered heritage site or a fabulous restaurant that you simply want to shout about. Whatever it might be, you can log on to www.explorer publishing.com and fill in our reader response form.

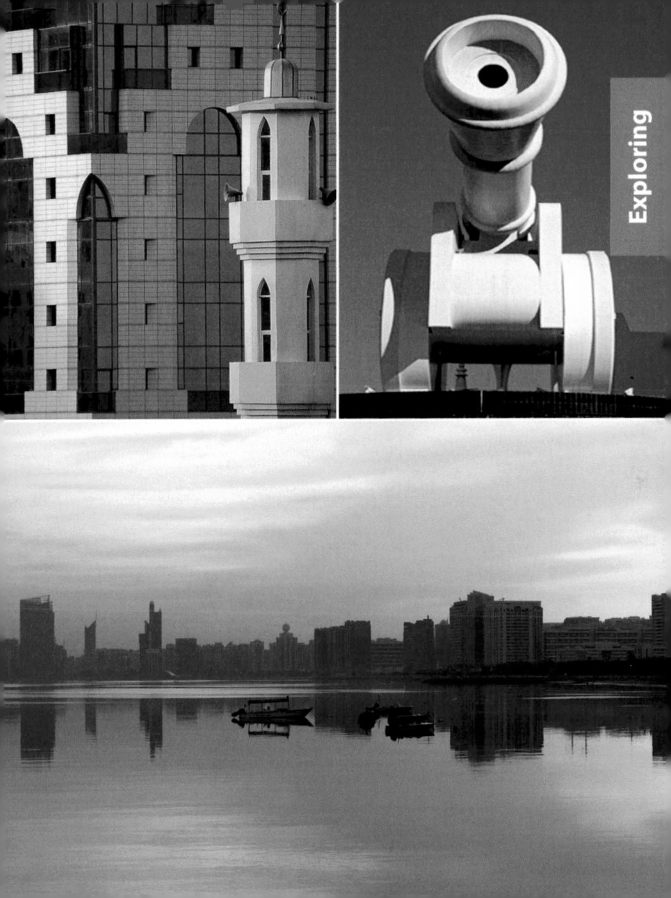

visitor's tour. It is packed with small shops selling everything from souvenirs to (not entirely authentic) designer label clothes. It's also a great place to test your bargaining skills.

The Madinat Zayed Shopping Centre & Gold Souk (p.136) is where a number of the shops from the old Central Souk have relocated to. It is quieter than the other big malls, but comes to life in the evenings. There are some bigger shops here, but it is especially worth a visit for the smaller shops selling perfumes, clothes, fabric and haberdashery.

The Gold Souk has some of the region's largest jewellery shops and is a great place to shop for gold (p.136). If you want

the classic souvenir of your name written in Arabic on a gold necklace, this is where to get it.

Some of the capital's top hotels are in this area, including Le Royal Meridien and the Sheraton Abu Dhabi Resort & Towers. While there are plenty of fine-dining restaurants within easy reach, don't miss out on the delicious authentic cuisine served at the many independent restaurants – good food at great prices, with a side order of atmosphere.

1 Qasr Al Hosn

Cultural Foundation, Shk Zayed First Street 02 619 5349

The Old Fort is the oldest building in Abu Dhabi, dating back to 1793, it was the official residence of the rulers of Abu Dhabi. The fort is part of the Cultural Foundation, and although it is not open to the public you can wander around the outside and get some great pictures. Currently it is under maintenance but will become a museum scheduled to open in 2009.

2 Cultural Foundation

Shk Zayed First Street www.cultural.org.ae/e 02 621 5300

This is Abu Dhabi's thriving community arts centre. It is located in the grounds of the Old Fort and is home to the National Library and the Institution of Culture and Art. Exhibitions, lectures and concerts are held regularly.

Timings: Sat to Wed: 8:00 to 14:00 & 17:00 to 21:00; Thu: 09:00 to 12:00 & 17:00 to 20:00; closed Fri.

Entrance: Adults Dhs.3, children Dhs.1.

Corniche East & Central Abu Dhabi

In the Area For...

One Hour

A stroll along the **corniche** is the ultimate way to tap into the heart of Abu Dhabi. When it's quiet you'll be able to appreciate the contrast between the landscaped greenery on one side and the bustling business district on the other. When it's busy you'll get to mingle with residents enjoying a bit of leisure time.

Half Day

After visiting the **Cultural Foundation** to explore the outside of **Qasr Al Hosn**, head down to the **Hamdan Centre** where you can practise the traditional art of bargaining and pick up some amazing souvenirs.

Full Day

Kick-start your day with a brisk walk along the **corniche**, then head up to the **Hamdan Centre** for a bit of shopping. Most shops in the area close for a long lunch at 13:00, so make your way to the top of the **Le Royal Meridien** to eat in the city's only revolving restaurant, Al Fanar. Squeeze in a quick visit to **Qasr Al Hosn** before heading for the **Gold Souk** – even if you're not buying, the sheer quantity of gold on offer is amazing. End the day with a cheap dinner at a pavement cafe, soaking up the atmosphere as the city starts winding down.

Al Meena & Tourist Club Area

AT THE NORTH-EASTERN TIP OF THE ISLAND ARE THE BUSTLING HIGH-RISE DISTRICTS. WITH SOME OF THE BEST HOTELS AND RECREATIONAL FACILITIES THAT THE CITY HAS TO OFFER, IT'S NO WONDER THAT THIS IS WHERE FUN-SEEKERS GATHER.

Al Meena is the name given to the whole of the north-eastern tip of Abu Dhabi island. The Tourist Club Area is an unofficial title given to the area from the Abu Dhabi Tourist Club to the Beach Rotana Hotel and down to Al Salam Street. Although the Tourist Club is currently closed for redevelopment, this bustling area is packed with high-rise apartment blocks, luxury hotels and some top shopping spots.

The Tourist Club Area's main draws are Abu Dhabi Mall (p.136) for its great shopping, multi-screen cinema and cafes; the Abu Dhabi Co-operative Complex (p.138), for more chances to shop; and the Khalifa Centre (just behind the old Co-op) which is packed with souvenir shops.

Some of Abu Dhabi's top hotels are in this area. They are known for their great restaurants and bars making the streets around them very popular

Top Scores
What's your flavour?

Culture	•••
Shopping	•••••
Sun	•••
Luxury	•••
Budget	•••
Kids	••••

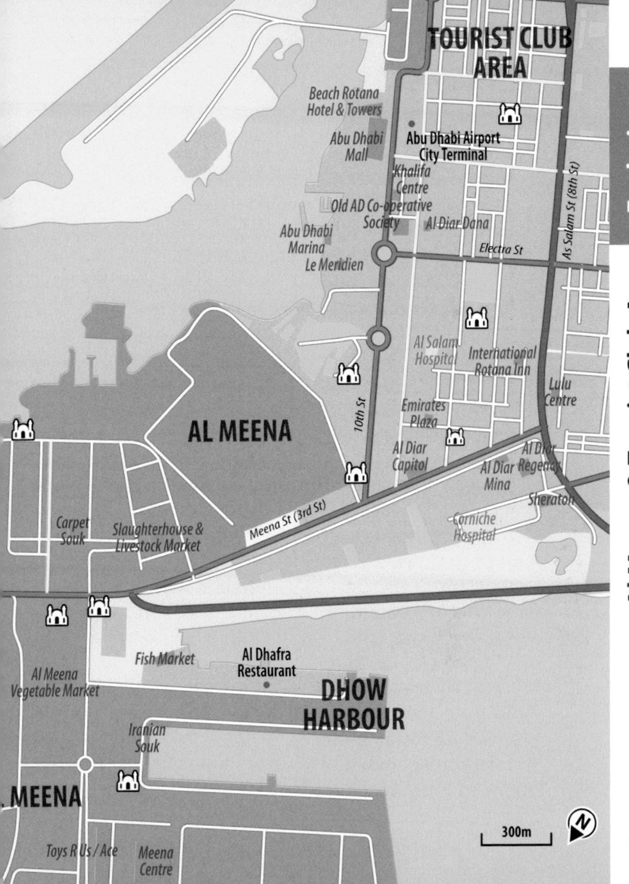
TOURIST CLUB AREA
Beach Rotana Hotel & Towers
Abu Dhabi Mall
Abu Dhabi Airport City Terminal
Khalifa Centre
Old AD Co-operative Society
Al Diar Dana
Abu Dhabi Marina Le Meridien
Electra St
As Salam St (8th St)
Al Salam Hospital
International Rotana Inn
Lulu Centre
10th St
Emirates Plaza
AL MEENA
Al Diar Capitol
Al Diar Mina
Al Diar Regency
Sheraton
Corniche Hospital
Meena St (3rd St)
Carpet Souk
Slaughterhouse & Livestock Market
Fish Market
Al Dhafra Restaurant
Al Meena Vegetable Market
DHOW HARBOUR
Iranian Souk
MEENA
Toys R Us / Ace
Meena Centre
300m
N

in the evenings (for more information, see Going Out, p.148). The Beach Rotana Hotel & Towers is linked to Abu Dhabi Mall – very handy if you're weighed down with shopping bags – and is home to the ever popular Trader Vics (p.189) as well as many other great restaurants. The Culinary Village at Le Meridien, just down the road also has a number of good restaurants (p.179) – you can choose between French, Indian or excellent Italian at Pappagallo (p.185) with its picturesque terrace.

Abu Dhabi Airport City Terminal is across the road from the Beach Rotana Hotel. Buses leave from here on a regular basis to Abu Dhabi International Airport and most airlines have check in facilities here too.

Al Meena begins as an area of high-rises and ends at Port Zayed (a working port). Once you leave the high-rises behind, the area on the right is best known for the Carpet Souk (p.144). Most of what is sold is mass-produced but there are gems to be found if you know what you're looking for. The Club, one of the capital's most popular health and beach clubs, is also here but unfortunately is for members only.

To the left, past the Customs building, is Port Zayed. This working port is home to the Fish Souk (p.146) – the odours emanating from here can politely be described as 'colourful'. The adjacent Vegetable Souk is probably

Picture Perfect

***Images of Abu Dhabi and the UAE*, available in leading bookshops and supermarkets, captures the awe-inspiring wonders of the city, from the architectural marvels to the breathtaking landscapes. It's a perfect memento of your holiday.**

a more pleasantly fragrant way to experience the hustle and bustle of a traditional market (p.146). Further on, you can browse through an impressive range of goods imported directly from Iran at the aptly named Iranian Souk. The Mina Centre, in the heart of the port, is a huge mall with a great bookshop (Jarir Bookstore), a supermarket, a children's amusement centre and a crazy-golf course.

The dhow harbour is particularly atmospheric at sunset when the fleet returns. The harbour is also the starting point for a number of dinner cruises, with the one run by the Al Dhafra seafood restaurant (p.180) being very popular – it sails along the corniche every evening.

Even though there are some beautiful sights in the port, no photography is allowed in the area as Port Zayed is a working port with security restrictions in place.

Exploring

Al Meena & Tourist Club Area

In the Area For...

One Hour

Pay a visit to the **Iranian Souk**, which is crammed full of stalls selling everything from household goods and terracotta urns to decorative metal and glass items.

Half Day

Peruse the catch of the day at the **Fish Market** before browsing through the myriad of colours and shapes at the **Vegetable Market**. Select a carpet at the nearby **Carpet Souk** and then head down to the **Dhow Harbour** to soak up the atmosphere created by traditional wooden dhows and their exotic cargos.

Full Day

Hit the retail jackpot with a trip around the many shops inside the **Abu Dhabi Mall**, one of the largest in Abu Dhabi. With four storeys, over 200 outlets and around 26,000 visitors daily, this is an essential destination if you like shopping. Relax afterwards at the adjacent **Beach Rotana Hotel & Towers** and enjoy a delicious buffet lunch at Rosebuds Restaurant & Terrace. Spend your afternoon exploring the souks: the **Iranian Souk**, the **Carpet Souk** and the **Fish and Vegetable Markets**, before setting sail from the **Dhow Harbour** for a relaxing **dinner cruise** organised by **Al Dhafra Seafood Restaurant**.

Al Safarat, Al Matar & Al Maqtaa

FORMING THE SOUTHERN END OF THE ISLAND, THESE AREAS BOAST SOME OF ABU DHABI'S MOST ICONIC LANDMARKS. HERE YOU CAN EXPLORE THE EMIRATE'S HERITAGE AND LOOK TO ITS FUTURE.

This end of the island is currently undergoing major development, with several tourist, residential and commercial projects under way. Al Safarat is dominated by the Abu Dhabi National Exhibition Centre (ADNEC), a newly re-developed purpose-built facility used for local and international events. These include the biennial International Defence Exhibition (IDEX), one of the largest exhibitions of its kind in the world. The authorities have identified the conference and exhibition sector as a key priority for future development and ADNEC's state-of-the art venues are expected to attract many major international business events. The area is also home to a number of embassies and Zayed Sports City, which has a football stadium, ice rink and bowling alley, access to the ice rink costs only Dhs.5, call 02 444 8458 for more info.

Old Airport Garden, near Zayed Sports City, is a lovely, established park with lots of shade and loads for kids to do. One

Top Scores
What's your flavour?

Culture	••••
Shopping	••
Sun	•••
Luxury	••
Budget	••
Kids	••••

Mussaffah Bridge
Armed Forces Officers Club & Hotel
AL MAQTAA
Maqtaa Fort
Eastern Ring Rd (8th St)
4
Sheikh Zayed Grand Mosque
AL MAQTAA
Coast Rd (30th St)
Ministry of Interior
Airport Rd (2nd St)
Bowling Hall
2
Sheikh Khalifa Park
UAE Football Federation
Old Airport Garden
1
Zayed Sports City
Ministry of Foreign Affairs
AL SAFARAT
Abu Dhabi Tourism Authority
General Secretariat of Municipalities
Carrefour
Sharia Court
Eastern Ring Rd (8th St)
AL MATAR
National Archives
33rd St
Al Bateen Airport
International Exhibition Centre
Abu Dhabi National Exhibition Centre
Zayed Military Hospital
Airport Rd (2nd St)
Public Garden
31st St
500m
N

side of the park is home to a few swings and small tidy gardens while the other side has an interesting and ornamental display.

Al Matar, on the other side of Airport Road, is dominated by the Sheikh Khalifa Park. This is one of the city's newest parks and a major landmark. The gardens have an international flavour and are set amid canals, fountains, lakes and waterfalls – not really what you'd expect with the desert on the doorstep. There are play areas for children and picnic spots, making this a popular place to get some fresh air, play a spot of frisbee or cricket in the open spaces or just relax with an ice cream and watch the world go by. Abu Dhabi is justifiably proud of its parks and this is one of the best.

Al Maqtaa is named after the heavily renovated Al Maqtaa Fort, which stands guard over the island. This area is dominated by the Sheikh Zayed bin Sultan Al Nahyan Mosque, known locally as the Grand Mosque, and the Armed Forces Officers Club & Hotel. The massive mosque, which will hold up to 10,000 worshippers, is nearing completion and is a major landmark. Although visitors are not allowed into the mosque, it does make for an impressive photo. The Armed Forces Officers Club & Hotel

Wanting More?

If the essential information on Abu Dhabi and its surrounding areas in this mini guide has left you wanting to know more about the exciting emirate then you're in luck. The *Abu Dhabi Explorer* is a Complete Residents' Guide, packed with even more information on exploring the city, including the best places to eat, drink and shop, as well as great places to stay and activities for families.

has some excellent recreational facilities, including two indoor shooting galleries and a good selection of restaurants.

1 Zayed Sports City

Al Safarat 02 444 8458

Zayed Sports City is a huge complex with a football stadium and an ice rink. The ice rink is one of the best places to go to beat the summer heat, but there are also a variety of other facilities including bumper cars, video games and a fast-food restaurant.

2 Sheikh Khalifa Park

Nr Al Bateen Airport, Al Matar

This landmark park has gardens set in a landscape of canals, fountains, lakes and waterfalls. Train tours of the park are available if you don't want to cover it on foot. It is home to kids' playgrounds, picnic facilities and an outdoor auditorium, and is popular in the evenings and at weekends.

3 Al Maqtaa Fort

Al Maqtaa

The 200 year-old, heavily renovated fort stands at the edge of the island and was built to fend off bandits. It is one of the few remaining of its kind in Abu Dhabi and provides a wonderful contrast to the modern bridge.

4 Sheikh Zayed bin Sultan Al Nahyan Mosque

Al Maqtaa

Known locally as the Grand Mosque, it will be able to hold up to 10,000 worshippers at any one time when it's finished, and is where Sheikh Zayed is buried. A hugely impressive landmark as you enter the island, it makes for a fantastic photo.

Al Safarat, Al Matar & Al Maqtaa

In the Area For...

One Hour

Depending on what time of year you visit Abu Dhabi you may want to escape the heat for a while. You can do so by heading down to **Zayed Sports City**, where you can and the kids can enjoy a spot of ice skating, bumper cars, video games and a whole host of fast food joints.

Half Day

Explore the outside of **Sheikh Zayed Grand Mosque**, which on completion will be able to hold up to 10,000 worshippers. Head over to the nearby **Sheikh Khalifa Park** for a leisurely stroll through lush greenery, before stopping for a bite at one of the independent street restaurants in the area.

Full Day

Visit **Sheikh Khalifa Park** for a morning stroll around the landscaped gardens and tranquil waterfalls and lakes. Then visit the **Sheikh Zayed Grand Mosque** to take some photos of the exterior of this impressive structure. Enjoy a delicious lunch at the **Armed Forces Officers Club & Hotel**, spend the afternoon ice skating at **Zayed Sports City**, then head for the **Maqtaa Bridge** for some early evening sunset photos of the 200 year old **Maqtaa Fort**.

Al Ain

WITH ITS NATURALLY FERTILE LAND AND ABUNDANCE OF GREENERY, AL AIN IS KNOWN AS 'THE GARDEN CITY'. THIS LUSH OASIS CITY LIES IN THE SHADOW OF THE CRAGGY JEBEL HAFEET MOUNTAIN AND IS SURROUNDED BY IMPOSING RED SAND DUNES.

Al Ain is the capital of the eastern region and Abu Dhabi emirate's second city. Its greenery and the fact that it is the birthplace and childhood home of Sheikh Zayed bin Sultan Al Nahyan, the former (and much-loved) ruler of the UAE, gives it special status in the hearts and minds of the people.

Today it only takes an hour and a half to drive from Abu Dhabi to Al Ain, but in the days before the discovery of oil, the journey took five days by camel. Most tour companies offer excursions to this fascinating city that straddles the border with the Sultanate of Oman; the UAE side is known as Al Ain and the Oman side as Buraimi.

The fortresses around the city, 18 in all, illustrate Al Ain's importance as part of the ancient trade route from Oman to the Arabian Gulf and there is evidence of the area having been inhabited for at least the last 7,000 years.

Top Scores

What's your flavour?

Culture	●●●●●
Shopping	●●●
Sun	●●
Luxury	●●
Budget	●●●
Kids	●●●●

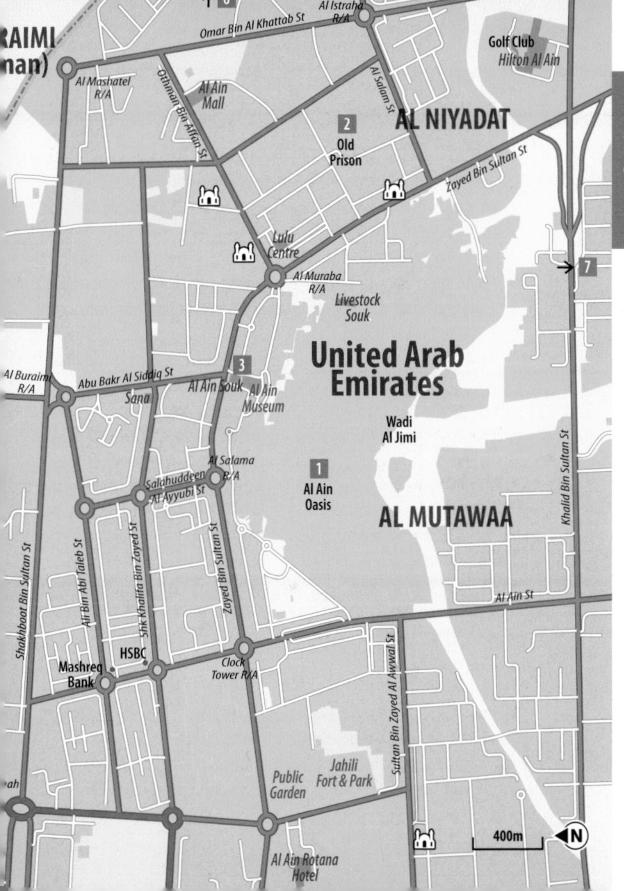
AIMI
nan)
Omar Bin Al Khattab St
Al Istraha R/A
Golf Club
Hilton Al Ain
Al Mashatel R/A
Othman Bin Affan St
Al Ain Mall
Al Salam St
AL NIYADAT
2
Old Prison
Zayed Bin Sultan St
Lulu Centre
Al Muraba R/A
Livestock Souk
7
United Arab Emirates
3
Al Buraimi R/A
Abu Bakr Al Siddiq St
Al Ain Souk
Al Ain Museum
Sana
Wadi Al Jimi
Al Salama R/A
Salahuddeen Al Ayyubi St
1
Al Ain Oasis
AL MUTAWAA
Khalid Bin Sultan St
Shakhboot Bin Sultan St
Ali Bin Abi Taleb St
Shk Khalifa Bin Zayed St
Zayed Bin Sultan St
Al Ain St
HSBC
Mashreq Bank
Clock Tower R/A
Sultan Bin Zayed Al Awwal St
Public Garden
Jahili Fort & Park
Al Ain Rotana Hotel
400m
N

Throughout his life, Sheikh Zayed pursued his vision of creating an oasis of greenery in the desert by initiating a series of 'greening' projects. As a result, Al Ain's seven natural oases are now surrounded by tree-lined streets and beautiful urban parks. The main Al Ain Oasis is home to palm plantations, many of which are working farms. The palms provide welcome shade and a haven from the noise and bustle of the city. Most of the farms still use the ancient falaj system of irrigation, which taps into underground water. If you do go exploring in the palm plantations, it is best to stick to the paved areas that weave between the walled-in farms. The Old Prison is also worth a visit simply for the stunning view of the surrounding town and oasis. The structure is a lone square turret in the centre of a gravel courtyard, surrounded by high walls. Unfortunately admittance is a bit hit and miss but if you visit as part of a tour you should be able to get in .

Al Ain's unique archaeological heritage and history is displayed at Al Ain Museum, on the edge of the main Al Ain Oasis. The museum has an interesting collection of photographs along with Bedouin jewellery, musical instruments, and a reconstruction of a traditional

Off-Road UAE

The UAE has some wonderfully contrasting landscapes that are well worth checking out, and the best way is by 4WD. If you're an outdoors type you should get your hands on the best-selling *UAE Off-Road Explorer*, which has 18 exciting off-road routes through desert, mountains and wadis, as well as info on places to see along the way.

majlis. The archaeological section houses many of the finds from nearby Hili Gardens and it's helpful to visit the museum before heading out to the gardens. The gift section houses an unusual collection of items that Sheikh Zayed received during his lifetime, including golden swords and a golden palm tree.

Al Ain is home to the last camel market of its kind in the UAE. The market is a great place to get up close and personal with the 'ships of the desert'. It is always busy and the exciting atmosphere builds up as traders discuss the value of each animal. You'll be able to get some great pictures to take home with you, but remember to ask permission before clicking.

Buraimi is part of the Sultanate of Oman but you won't need a visa to enter. The Buraimi Souk buzzes with local colour and atmosphere, and you'll find a few souvenir shops selling pottery, silver jewellery and woven carpets. The Al Hilli Fort, behind the souk, is a good starting point for exploring the Buraimi Oasis. The Al Khandaq Fort, located in the town of Hamasa in Buraimi, is thought to be around 400 years old (although it has been restored). There are some amazing views to be had from the battlements.

Al Ain's biggest attraction, literally, is Jebel Hafeet. At 1,180

Jebel Hafeet

Rising abruptly from the surrounding countryside, Jebel Hafeet dominates the area and the views from the top are simply unmissable. On a clear day you can see the surrounding desert plains, oases, wadis and the Hajar Mountain range in the distance. The road to the top is in excellent condition with a number of strategic viewpoints along the way.

metres, the views from the top of this mountain are spectacular. If you are looking for a room with a view, the five-star Mercure Grand Hotel, at 915m, will give you a bird's eye view of the desert plains below.

The Green Mubazzarah Park is at the foot of the mountain, and is home to hot springs, swimming pools and numerous chalets. It is extremely popular at weekends.

Al Ain Zoo is one of the Gulf region's better and larger zoos, stretching over 400 hectares. The layout is a bit confusing but you can pick up a map at the entrance. The zoo has a special breeding programme for endangered species.

1 Al Ain Oasis

Nr Al Ain Museum 03 763 0155

The area is divided into palm plantations, many of which are working farms. Visit this cool, tranquil area to see the ancient falaj system of irrigation, which draws water from underground. Other oases include the Al Gattara Oasis which has a heritage village.

2 Green Mubazzarah

Nr Jebel Hafeet 03 783 9555

At the base of the imposing Jebel Hafeet mountain are the hot springs of Green Mubazzarah. They are a grand spot to rest and paddle in the supposedly curative waters.

3 Al Ain Museum

Al Muraba R/A www.aam.gov.ae 03 764 1595

This museum, on the edge of the main Al Ain Oasis, has exhibits on the archaeology of the area, the culture and heritage of the people, and a selection of gifts received by Sheikh Zayed during his lifetime.

4 Hili Archaeological Gardens

Mohammed Bin Khalifa St

The gardens are 10km outside Al Ain, on the Dubai road. The area includes both an archaeological site and a public garden. There are remnants from a Bronze Age settlement (2500 – 2000BC), excavated and restored in 1995, and a number of the artefacts found are on display at the museum.

5 Hili Fun City & Ice Rink

Mohammed Bin Khalifa St 03 784 5542

There are over 30 rides in this amusement park, including carousels and rollercoasters. It also has picnic spots, food outlets and souvenir shops. The ice rink is next door.

Timings: **(Winter)** Sat – Wed: 16:00 – 22:00, Fri and public holidays 09:00 – 22:00. **(Summer)** Sat – Wed 17:00 – 22:00; Fri and public holidays 09:00 – 22:00. Thu 17:00 – 23:00. Tue & Wed women & children only. Closed Sun.

6 Camel Market

Nr Town Centre

This is the last of its kind in the UAE. A visit to this market is a fantastic way to mingle with locals and experience trading as it has taken place for centuries. Hearing the excited owners discussing the virtues and values of their prize camels will give you a newfound respect for these ungainly (yet surprisingly expensive) animals. Open mornings only.

7 Al Ain Zoo & Aquarium

Nr Jebel Hafeet 03 782 8188

Stretching over 400 hectares, this is one of the largest and best zoos in the Gulf region. Because of its size, and the somewhat confusing layout, it is best to pick up a free map at the entrance. This is your chance to get up close to some rare and common local species such as the Arabian Oryx and gazelles. A train departs from the central concourse every 15 minutes, providing a whirlwind tour of the zoo. At time of writing, the aquarium was closed for refurbishment.

Entrance: Dhs.10; children under four years, free.

Winter Timings (October to April): 08:00 to 17:30

Summer Timings (May to September): 16:00 to 23:00

Al Ain

In the Area For...

One Hour

Spend a dreamy hour surrounded by palm trees in the tranquil shade of the **Al Ain Oasis**. Many of the palm plantations are still working farms so you can see the ancient falaj irrigation system in action.

Half Day

See haggling at its best at the **Camel Market**, then catch up with Al Ain's unique archaeology and history in the **Al Ain Museum**, situated on the edge of the main oasis. The collection of photographs taken in the 60s is particularly interesting. Head over to the **Hili Archaeological Gardens** where you can learn more about some of the museum's artefacts and where they were excavated.

Full Day

Get a bird's eye view of the surrounding town and oasis with a visit to the **Old Prison** and then explore the **palm plantations** on foot (stick to the paved areas). Head out towards **Jebel Hafeet**, stopping at the bottom to dip your toes in the hot springs of **Green Mubazzarah**, before driving to the summit (1,180m) to enjoy spectacular views. Pop into the **Mercure Grand Hotel** for lunch on the terrace. Call into the **Al Ain Zoo**, then enjoy a traditional night of Arabic food and entertainment in Al Dana at the **Hotel InterContinental**.

Other Attractions

FROM TRADITIONAL SPORTS TO TRIPS THROUGH THE MOUNTAINS, THESE PAGES ARE PACKED WITH REASONS TO LEAVE THE SUN LOUNGER BEHIND AND DISCOVER THE WONDERS OF THIS DIVERSE COUNTRY.

Camel Racing

Despite their ungainly appearance, camels can reach surprisingly high speeds. Race meetings are held on Friday and Saturday mornings between October and March, from around 07:30. Al Maqam Camel Race Track, about 45km outside Abu Dhabi on the road to Al Ain, is the closest to the city.

Falconry

Falconry is part of the UAE's history and remains an important part of Abu Dhabi's culture and traditions. The best way to see the birds in flight is to visit the Breakwater Heritage Village where displays are held on Thursday evenings during the summer months.

Horse Racing

Horse racing is a huge sport in the UAE and is enjoyed by residents and visitors alike. Race meetings are held in the evenings during the winter, where you can see some of the world's top jockeys and horses in action (see www.emiratesracing.com for the calendar). There's no betting, but 'pick-the-winner' competitions are popular and feature some great prizes. Admission is usually free.

Parks & Beaches

Abu Dhabi is surprisingly lush for a desert city and is well known for its public parks. The city's most notable parks are the corniche and Sheikh Khalifa Park.

There are several public beaches, mainly in the Ras Al Akhdar area. No cars are allowed on the beaches, but jetskis are permitted, so take care when swimming. Al Raha Beach, on the road to Dubai, is undergoing extensive development which will include a number of parks with various family-friendly facilities.

Corniche Cruises & Island Tours

Several companies offer cruises along the corniche or out to the islands, including Blue Dolphin Company (02 666 9392) and Sunshine Tours (02 444 9914). If you want to see the city from a different perspective, this is the way to do it.

The Shuja Yacht (02 695 0539) (p.156) is operated by Le Royal Meridien. Enjoy a delicious meal as the sun sets and you slip gently past the bustle of the city.

Futaisi Island (02 666 6601) is famed for its wildlife, including some rare species, an authentic Arabian fort, a traditional mosque and mangrove lagoon.

Powerboats

For those who are interested in seeing boats move at a more rapid pace, the Abu Dhabi International Marine Sports Club (www.adimsc.com) hosts the international Formula One and Formula 2000 championships. These events draw big crowds to the corniche.

Tours

AN ORGANISED TOUR CAN BE A GREAT WAY OF DISCOVERING THE UAE, ESPECIALLY IF YOU'RE ONLY HERE FOR A SHORT TIME. WHETHER YOU PREFER ACTIVITIES, SIGHTSEEING OR SHOPPING, YOU'LL FIND A TOUR TO SUIT YOU.

Whether you've only got a spare half day, or you want to camp overnight in the desert, you can find a tour that fits in with your timings. Most tours need to be booked in advance and most tour operators visit the main hotels in order to book tours for guests. However, some tours may need to be booked further in advance with your travel agent, especially if they involve travel to another emirate.

City Tours – In Abu Dhabi

Abu Dhabi Tour

This tour takes in the city's main landmarks from the corniche to the Cultural Foundation, Dhow Harbour, Heritage Village and the Women's Handicraft Centre (half day).

City Tours – Out of Abu Dhabi

Dubai City Tour

Enjoy old Dubai with visits to the Gold Souk, Bastakiya and Dubai Museum. Take a ride on an abra, then head for the striking, modern malls, where you may even have time for some shopping (full day).

Ajman & Sharjah Tour

Visit the working dhow yards in Ajman before exploring the famous museums and souks of Sharjah (full day).

Al Ain Tour

The oasis city of Al Ain is full of history, from the 4,000 year-old tombs at Hili to the 175 year-old Al Nahyan family fort and the UAE's only remaining traditional camel market (full day).

Liwa Tour

The five-hour trip from Abu Dhabi to Liwa Oasis is well worth the effort. Spectacular sand dunes, scattered villages and the vast emptiness of the Empty Quarter are awe-inspiring.

Ras Al Khaimah Tour

Travel up the 'pirate coast' to the oldest seaport in the region to visit Ras Al Khaimah museum and the old town, before returning via the starkly beautiful Hajar Mountains (full day).

Safari Tours

Dune Dinners

Enjoy the thrill of some hair-raising dune driving, followed by a desert sunset and a sumptuous buffet. You'll also enjoy camel rides, henna painting and belly dancing.

East Coast

The scenery of the east coast is spectacular and on an organised tour you'll see the oldest mosque in the UAE and the Friday markets, which actually open every day (full day).

Full Day Safari

This tour usually passes through traditional Bedouin villages and camel farms in the desert en route to dunes of varying colours and heights. Most tours also visit Fossil Rock and the stark and majestic Hajar Mountains.

Hatta Pools Safari

The remarkable Hatta Pools in the Hajar Mountains are a must-see. This tour usually includes lunch at the Hatta Fort Hotel, although in the cooler months some tour groups may prefer to stop for lunch in the mountains (full day).

Mountain Safari

Taking in some of the most outstanding scenery in the country, you'll head north to Ras Al Khaimah before travelling through the Hajar Mountains near Wadi Bih to Dibba. Your route will take you past terraced mountainsides and stone houses at over 1,200 metres above sea level. You'll leave the mountains at Dibba and return to Abu Dhabi on the highway. Some tours start at Dibba (full day).

Overnight Safari

Starting at around 15:00 with a drive through the dunes to a Bedouin-style campsite, you'll dine under the stars and sleep in the fresh air. Many tours include entertainment such as belly dancing and traditional music. The morning drive heads for the mountains before heading back to the city.

Other Emirates

EACH EMIRATE HAS ITS OWN DISTINCT CHARACTER. DUBAI IS A GLITZY TOURIST HOTSPOT, SHARJAH IS THE UNDISPUTED CULTURAL CAPITAL, AND FUJAIRAH IS HOME TO BREATHTAKINGLY BEAUTIFUL LANDSCAPES.

The six other emirates which make up the UAE lie to the north of Abu Dhabi and only occupy 13% of the country's landmass. Dubai, Sharjah, Ajman, Umm Al Qaiwain, and Ras Al Khaimah lie on the west coast, with Fujairah on the east coast. If your stay in Abu Dhabi is long enough to permit exploration of the other emirates, you should definitely make the effort to see their unique characteristics.

Dubai

Dubai is the place that the whole world is talking about. Although it is a super-busy construction hotspot, it is still a fascinating city to visit. Among all the cranes and almost-completed high-rises you'll find a selection of the world's most luxurious hotels, some amazing leisure facilities (an indoor ski slope, with real snow, to name just one) and several stunning beaches.There are also a number of world renowned events worth checking out, including the IRB Rugby Sevens in December, the Tennis Championship in Februrary/March, The World Cup horse racing in March and golf's Dubai Desert Classic, also in March. And then of course there's the shopping, which is among the best in the world.

Dubai Checklist

Dubai Museum	www.dubaitourism.ae
Bastakiya Heritage Area	
Heritage & Diving Village	www.dubaitourism.ae
Abra Ride (Water Taxi)	
Gold Souk	
Spice Souk	
Jumeira Mosque	www.cultures.ae
World class shopping malls	
Ski Dubai at Mall of the Emirates	www.skidxb.com
Wild Wadi Water Park	www.wildwadi.com
WonderLand Theme & Water Park	www.wonderlanduae.com

Hatta

Still part of the emirate of Dubai, Hatta is a small town on the edge of the Hajar Mountains near the UAE-Oman border. It is famous for the Hatta Pools, deep canyons carved out by rushing floodwater. A traditional mountain village has been recreated at the Hatta Heritage Village, and the tranquil Hatta Fort Hotel is a great escape from the city.

Sharjah

Although infamous for its traffic congestion, Sharjah is a fascinating place that should be on every visitor's itinerary. In 1998, Unesco named Sharjah the cultural capital of the Arab World for its commitment to art, culture and preserving its traditional heritage. The museums are very well presented

and the souks have a more authentic feel than many in other emirates. Sharjah is the only emirate with territory on both the west and east coasts. If you get to see both coasts, you'll appreciate the contrast between bustling city and attractive beaches on the west, and beautiful mountains and lagoons on the east. The website www.sharjah-welcome.com contains information on all the attractions listed below.

Sharjah Checklist

- **Sharjah Heritage Area**
- **Sharjah Heritage Museum**
- **Qanat Al Qasba**
- **Sharjah Archaeological Museum**
- **Sharjah Art Museum**
- **Sharjah Islamic Museum**
- **Sharjah Maritime Museum**
- **Sharjah Science Museum**
- **Sharjah Natural History Museum**
- **Arabian Wildlife Centre**
- **Discovery Centre**
- **Blue Souk**
- **Souk Al Arsah**

Ajman

Ajman is the smallest emirate, with some good beaches and a corniche. It's home to some of the region's largest dhow building yards and the old souk, both of which will take you back in time to a more simple way of life. The Ajman Kempinski Hotel is a good stopover for lunch or dinner while in Ajman.

Umm Al Qaiwain

Umm Al Qaiwain (UAQ) is a quiet emirate where life hasn't changed much over the years. But quiet doesn't necessarily mean boring, since the sheltered waters of the large lagoon are popular for watersports, and UAQ is home to flying clubs, shooting clubs and car racing associations. The natural mangroves also attract an abundance of local wildlife.

One of the emirate's most popular attractions is Dreamland Aqua Park (06 768 1888, www.dreamlanduae.com). With water rides to suit people of all ages and courage-levels, a go-kart track, a variety of cafes and restaurants, and a licensed pool bar, there's loads to do. Umm Al Quwain is full of quiet camping spots, so if you're too tired to head back to Abu Dhabi, you can set up camp and sleep under the stars.

Ras Al Khaimah

Ras Al Khaimah (RAK) is the most northern of the seven emirates, and boasts what is probably the best scenery in the country. It sits between the Hajar mountains and the Arabian Gulf, so on one side you see stunning mountain vistas and on the other tranquil waters and white sandy beaches.

The souk in the old town and the National Museum of Ras Al Khaimah are worth visiting. The museum is housed in an old fort and, as well as displays of jewellery and local archaeological finds, it has an account of the British naval expedition against RAK in 1809. Look out for fossils in the rock strata of the walls of the fort; they date back 190 million years.

The town is a good starting point for exploring the mountains and is the entry point to the amazing Mussandam Peninsula in Oman.

East Coast

Even if you're only in the UAE for a short time, a trip over to the east coast is well worth the effort. The area is popular with outdoor enthusiasts, with craggy mountains perfect for rock climbing, and clear, calm waters perfect for diving or snorkelling (see the ***UAE Underwater Explorer*** for more information). The main settlements along the coast begin at Dibba, the starting or finishing point of the stunning drive through Wadi Bih. Badiyah is home to the oldest mosque in the UAE (it is still used for prayer so non-Muslims are not allowed inside). Khor Fakkan (part of Sharjah), has some of the area's best dive sites just minutes from the coast, and the Al Hisn Fort in Kalba houses the town's museum.

Ras Al Khaimah joined the other six emirates in the UAE in 1972, a month after the creation of the federation. It is the only city on the east coast. The fort overlooking the town is around 300 years old and with other forts and watchtowers in the surrounding hills, the area has an air of mystery and charm. The busy modern port is the UAE's access to the Indian Ocean. The museum houses displays of local artefacts and archaeological finds. The area between the Hilton Hotel and Khor Kalba still hosts the traditional sport of 'bull butting' on Friday afternoons during the winter. The sport consists of two huge bulls going head-to-head for several rounds (it is not a blood sport and shouldn't be confused with Spanish bullfighting).

The mountain village of Bithna, on the road from Fujairah to Sharjah, is best known for its fort and archaeological site. The fort once controlled the main pass through the mountains and is still impressive. The archaeological site is thought to have been a communal burial site dating from 1350BC to 300BC, and there is a detailed display of the tomb in Fujairah Museum.

At the southern end of the east coast, on the border with Oman, are Kalba and Khor Kalba. Kalba is part of Sharjah and is renowned for its mangrove forest and golden beaches. It is a pretty fishing village that has retained much of its historical charm. Further to the south is the village of Khor Kalba, the site of the northernmost mangrove forest in the world. It is home to a unique variety of plants, birds and marine life. On the spring and autumn migration routes, it's the only breeding site for the rare white-collared kingfisher. If you are lucky, you may also get to see a few turtles swimming in the lagoon. Desert Rangers (www.desertrangers.com) offers a canoe tour through the reserve (the tour leaves from Dubai).

Tour Operators

ORGANISED TOURS ARE OFFERED BY A NUMBER OF COMPANIES IN ABU DHABI AND AL AIN. YOUR HOTEL'S CONCIERGE SHOULD HAVE INFORMATION ON WHICH TOURS ARE AVAILABLE AND MAY EVEN BE ABLE TO GET YOU A SPECIAL DEAL. IF NOT, CONTACT THE COMPANIES BELOW AND GET OUT AND EXPLORE THIS FASCINATING COUNTRY.

Abdul Jalil Travel Agency

Liwa Street (Al Markaziyah)
Phone: 02 622 5225 Fax: 02 622 7395 Email: aljta001@eim.ae

Abu Dhabi Travel Bureau

Corniche Road, next to Chamber of Commerce
Phone: 02 633 8700 Fax: 02 634 6020 Email: atb@eim.ae

Advanced Travel & Tourism

Hamdan Street (Al Markaziyah)
Phone: 02 634 7900 Fax: 02 632 5334 Email: advantvl@eim.ae

Al Ain Golden Sands Camel Safaris

Hilton Al Ain
Phone: 03 768 8006 Fax: 03 768 8005

Al Mahboob Travel

PO Box: 18416, Al Ain
Phone: 03 751 5944 Fax: 03 751 5584 Email: almahboob@eim.ae

Al Toofan Travel & Tours

Khalifa Bin Zayed Street
Phone: 02 631 3515 Fax: 02 631 5055 Email: cyclone_t@hotmail.com

Arabian Adventures

Shk Hamdan Bin Mohammed Street
Phone: 02 691 1711 Fax: 02 691 1710 www.arabian-adventures.com

Emirates Holidays

Corniche Road
Phone: 02 691 1722 Fax: 02 691 1670 www.emirates-holidays.com

Emirates Travel Express

Main Street – next to Jumeira Studio
Phone: 03 765 0777 Fax: 03 751 5747 www.eteholidays.com

Gulf Travel Express

Nr Lulu Shopping Centre
Phone: 03 766 6737 Fax: 03 766 4744

Middle East Travel

Main Street, beh Habib Bank
Phone: 03 764 1661 Fax: 03 764 2478

Net Tours

Sheraton Abu Dhabi Resort & Towers
Phone: 02 679 4656 Fax: 02 671 1232 www.nettoursdubai.com

Offroad Emirates

Fourth Street, btn Shk Zayed 2nd St & Shk Hamdan Bin Mohammed St
Phone: 02 633 3232 Fax: 02 633 6642 www.offroademirates.com

Salem Travel Agency

Muroor Road, opp Madinat Zayed Shopping Centre
Phone: 02 621 8000 Fax: 02 621 1155 travels@salemtravelagency.com

Sunshine Tours

Airport Road, beh Carrefour, Abu Dhabi National Hotels building
Phone: 02 444 9914 Fax: 02 444 6856 Email: abusun@eim.ae

Thomas Cook Al Rostamani

Al Ghurair building, Shk Hamdan Bin Mohammed St
Phone: 02 672 7500 Fax: 02 672 8521 www.tcart-me.com

Sports & Spas

Sports

BEST KNOWN AS A SUN-SOAKED LUXURY DESTINATION, ABU DHABI OFFERS MUCH, MUCH MORE – WHETHER YOU'RE LOOKING FOR SPORTS AND ACTION OR JUST A SPOT OF RELAXATION AT ONE OF THE SPAS.

Visitors to Abu Dhabi are sure to be delighted by the wide variety of sports and activities available, from the wonderfully indulgent to the adrenalin fuelled. Winter (October to March) is the best time to enjoy outdoor activities (although many visitors enjoy such pursuits all year round), whether it's mainstream sports like golf and tennis or more extreme pursuits such as caving, mountain biking, rock climbing and skydiving. For those less keen on the summer heat, there are plenty of indoor activities available, and most hotels have excellent gym facilities, meanwhile the hardcore can still brave the daytime temperatures that regularly rise above 45°C. Just don't forget the high factor suncream.During the hotter months early mornings and late evenings are the best option for outdoor activities, be it watersports or a round of floodlit golf, or a relaxed walk along the corniche.

If you are interested in having a go at some of the adventure activities such as climbing, off-roading, mountain biking, dune buggying or quad biking, then there are a number of reputable tour operators (see p.106) that will able to offer tailored activity trips. In fact extreme sports enthusiasts from around the world travel to the UAE to experience its unique desert, wadi and mountainous terrain and breathtaking scenery.

Taking a trip out into the wilderness is a must, and there are various tours on offer (p.92). If you're feeling adventurous, places to see include the Rub Al Khali or 'Empty Quarter' (the last great frontier of uninhabited desert), the miraculous oases hidden among sand dunes or the dramatic wadis and

jagged mountains towering out of the desert. If you've got the confidence (and the insurance) and are in a group you can hire a 4WD and pick up a copy of the ***UAE Off-Road Explorer***, or alternatively join an organised tour.

Other active exploits on offer include canoeing at the Khor Kalba Nature Reserve on the UAE's east coast, where you can get close to the country's native bird and marine life. Tours are available from Desert Rangers (based in Dubai, www.desertrangers.com, 04 340 2408). Those keen on equine sports could visit the Ghantoot Racing and Polo Club (562 9050, www.emiratesracing.com).

Make Like a Local

If you're in town for more than a flying visit and want to check out what additional sports and activities are on offer then grab a copy of the *Abu Dhabi Explorer* Complete Residents' Guide. This indispensible guide to living in the city has a comprehensive activities chapter packed with information on every energetic (as well as relaxing) sport or activity that you can think of whether it's sea, sand or sky-based.

If activities and adventure don't fit in with your plans, then there's always the option of spectating instead. Abu Dhabi and its neighbour, Dubai, regularly offer a wide range of annual events from world-class tennis tournaments, golf, rugby, motorsports and sailing among the long list that draws the top names of the sporting elite (see annual events, p.212). Or for those true armchair sports fans there are various sports bars that show international events, such as the Hiltonia Sports Bar in the Hilton Al Ain or PJ O'Reilly's in Le Royal Meridien.

Watersports

IN THE COASTAL WATERS OFF ABU DHABI YOU'LL FIND A WIDE VARIETY OF WATERSPORTS ON OFFER. FROM SNORKELLING TO SAILING, EXPLORING THE ARABIAN GULF IS A MUST.

With an ideal climate and the beautiful warm waters of the Gulf on its doorstep, Abu Dhabi is a great location for watersports. Snorkelling equipment is available for hire at most hotels or dive centres. The Blue Dolphin Company in the Hotel InterContinental runs organised half-day excursions for Dhs.350 per person (02 666 9392). Alternatively you can hire a car and take a trip to Snoopy Island near the Sandy Beach Hotel in Dibba (where you can hire snorkelling gear). Located on the UAE's east coast it is one of the best locations for snorkelling and diving.

Other exhilarating watersports include parasailing, wakeboarding, skiing or even jetskiing, which is rapidly gaining popularity with the fun-loving people of the UAE. For non-motorised watersports you will not be disappointed as there is kayaking, kitesurfing, windsurfing, scuba diving, sailing and even some surfing (although in all honesty the waves are moderate at best in the sheltered Gulf seas).

The Gulf waters may appear a lot calmer than other seas but do not be deceived: they can be just as dangerous so common sense is necessary. You should be aware of hidden dangers such as jellyfish, stingrays, occasional strong currents and riptides. Popular beach parks will have a lifeguard's flag, so make sure you pay attention to it and if you're at one of the unguarded public beaches then be especially careful.

Diving

BALMY WEATHER, WARM SEAS AND REEFS CREATE THE PERFECT ENVIRONMENT FOR DISCOVERING THE UAE'S UNDERWATER WORLD AND FASCINATING COASTAL WILDLIFE. WHETHER YOU ARE A BEGINNER OR A SEASONED EXPERT, YOU'LL ENJOY THE GULF'S WATERS.

The waters around the UAE are rich in a variety of marine and coral life as well as several submerged wrecks (some deliberately sunk to form offshore reefs). The great thing about the location is that it is possible to dive all year round in the warm seas. In addition to exotic fish, such as clownfish and seahorses, you can see barracuda, spotted eagle rays, moray eels, small sharks, stingrays, sea turtles, and much more.

There are plenty of dive companies (see p.118) in the UAE offering all levels of courses, from introductory dives to instructor level and technical diving from international training organisations, such as CMAS, PADI and NAUI.

Many good dive sites are easily accessible from Abu Dhabi, including wreck or deep-water dives and reef dives. For shallow dives (eight metres), the Old Cement Barge is interesting while the popular deep dive sites are at Hannan, MS Jazim and MS Lion City. If you want to explore further around the UAE, the east coast is especially popular and is home to some stunning marine life. Most dive companies also organise trips to the spectacular area north of the UAE known as the Mussandam. Alternatively, from Dibba on the east coast, boats take divers as far up the coast as they desire. For further information on diving in the UAE and the Mussandam, refer to the ***UAE Underwater Explorer***, available at bookshops.

Licence to Dive

If you're a certified diver then always remember to pack your certification card as no dive organisation in the UAE will allow you to dive without one, unless you are undergoing a training course. For serious divers there are a number of marinas where you can moor your boat (for a fee).

UAE Dive Centres

7 Seas Divers www.7seasdivers.com
P.O. Box 9878, Khor Fakkan
Phone: 09 238 7400 Fax: 09 238 7440

Abu Dhabi Sub Aqua Club www.abudhabisubaqua.com
The Club, Al Meena
Phone: 02 673 1111 Fax: 02 673 1113

Arabian Divers www.fishabudhabi.com
Al Bateen Marina
Mobile: 050 614 6931 Fax: 02 665 8742

Al Jazira Dive Centre www.goldentulipaljazira.com
Al Diar Jazira Club
Phone: 02 562 9100 Fax: 02 562 9035

Blue Dolphin Company LLC padi_premier@yahoo.com
Hotel InterContinental, Bainuna St
Phone: 02 666 9392 Fax: 02 666 6802

Golden Boats golboat@eim.ae
Nr Central Bank Bld, Al Bateen
Phone: 02 666 9119 Fax: 02 666 9970

Sandy Beach Diving Centre sandybm@eim.ae
Fujairah
Phone: 09 244 5555/5354 Fax: 09 244 5200

Scuba 2000 www.scuba-2000.com
Al Bidiya Beach, Fujairah
Phone: 09 238 8477 Fax: 09 238 8478

Scuba International www.scubainternational.net
Fujairah
Phone: 09 220 0060 Fax: 09 222 0548

Sharjah Wanderers Dive Club www.sharjahwanderers.com
Samnan Area, Sharjah
Phone: 06 5662105 Fax: 06 566 3226

Golf

DESPITE ITS DESERT LOCATION THE UAE HAS SOME WORLD-CLASS GOLF COURSES WITH OUTSTANDING FACILITIES. IN ABU DHABI YOU CAN PLAY THE P.G.A. CHAMPIONSHIP COURSE OR, FOR A DIFFERENT CHALLENGE, YOU CAN ALWAYS TEST YOUR ALL-TERRAIN SKILLS ON A SAND COURSE.

Abu Dhabi is rapidly making its mark as a leading international golf destination. Global television coverage of the Abu Dhabi Golf Championship, a European PGA tour event attracting some of the leading names in international golf, is dramatically raising the emirate's profile among the world's golf enthusiasts. There are already a number of options available for the keen golfer and the future looks even brighter, as Abu Dhabi has plans to build several new courses of championship standard in the near future.

Abu Dhabi Golf Club by Sheraton 02 558 8990

Umm Al Nar St, Umm Al Nar, www.adgolfsheraton.com

Located just 30 minutes from the centre of city, this is the venue of the Abu Dhabi Golf Championship. The club's excellent facilities include the challenging 18-hole, 7,204 yard, par 72 National Course and the more forgiving 9 hole, 3,299 yard, par 36 Garden Course (2 x 9 available), a golf academy, 350 metre driving range and practice facilities. The falcon-shaped clubhouse also features restaurants, a pro-shop, pool, spa and tennis courts.

Abu Dhabi Golf & Equestrian Club
02 445 9600

Al Mushrif, www.adec-web.com

This par 70 course boasts one of the longest par five holes in the Gulf, at 630 yards. Although there are only nine holes, there are alternate tees for the back nine. Green fees for visitors are Dhs.230 for 18 holes and Dhs.140 for nine holes, with cart hire costing Dhs.40 for 18 holes and Dhs.25 for nine holes. Range balls cost Dhs.10 per bucket for members and Dhs.20 for non-members. Competitions are held each Friday.

Al Ain Golf Club
03 768 6808

Hotel InterContinental, Al Ain

The Al Ain Golf Club, east of the InterContinental Hotel, boasts an 18 hole sand course and a floodlit driving range. Handicaps gained here are valid internationally. Visitors are welcome, but should phone ahead. The sand is treated and compacted, creating a smooth surface that putts similar to a green.

Al Ghazal Golf Club

02 575 8040

Nr Abu Dhabi Intl Airport, www.alghazalgolf.ae

This purpose-built 18 hole sand golf course, driving range, academy and licensed clubhouse is situated two minutes from the capital's airport, and has hosted the World Sand Golf Championship. Anyone can play here, including transit passengers with a few hours to kill – airlines can arrange free 96-hour passenger transit visas for travellers who want to play golf or use the facilities.

Hilton Al Ain Golf Club

02 558 8990

Hilton Al Ain, Al Ain, www.al-ain.hilton.com

The holes of this par three course average about 80 yards in length but, though short, can be tough to play. The course has nearly 30 bunkers and very small quick greens. It is open to non-members, and lessons are available. There is an entrance fee of Dhs.10 for non-members and green fees are Dhs.30; club hire starts from Dhs.30 for a half set.

UAE Golf Association

04 399 5060

Emirates Golf Club, Dubai, www.ugagolf.com

This non-profit organisation is the governing body for amateur golf in the UAE. It is overseen by the General Authority of Youth & Sports and actively supports junior players and the development of the national team. The affiliate membership rate is Dhs.200 for a year, and the UGA Handicap Scheme costs Dhs.595. Members get a number of benefits, including a reduction in green fees. The website has a comprehensive calendar of forthcoming events.

Spas

ARABIAN LUXURY EXTENDS TO SPLENDID SPAS THAT WILL TRANSPORT YOU TO PAMPERING PARADISE. IF YOU WANT TO FEEL LIKE CLEOPATRA THEN YOU'VE COME TO THE RIGHT PLACE.

No luxury holiday is complete without a trip to the spa for a truly hedonistic head-to-toe pampering session. Abu Dhabi has its fair share of opulent hotels with equally magnificent spas. Whether you just fancy a facial or desire a day of indulgence you will find a wide variety of treatments on offer for the mind, body and face. From anti-ageing to body firming you will leave feeling like a new person. Unique to the region is the traditional Arabian treatment, the luxurious Hammam experience, involving a full-body henna mask and some serious scrubbing – definitely not one for the inhibited!

Eden Spa & Health Club 02 697 4254

Le Meridien, www.abudhabi.lemeridien.com

The ultimate in stress relief and personal pampering, treatments include sessions in the aquamedic pool, various massages, aromatherapies, facials, mineral baths, seaweed wraps, Turkish baths as well as their specialities of Lithos Therapy and Ayurveda. There is also a health club on-site, along with a tranquil beach and a variety of pools to relax in and around.

Hiltonia Health Club & Spa 02 681 1900

Hilton International Abu Dhabi, www.hilton.com

The Hiltonia Spa is a haven of tranquility in beautiful surroundings. Apart from the usual aromatherapy and reflexology treatments, they also offer Indian head massage and a range of hydro bath treatments. Alternatively you can choose from their menu of special treatment packages, which combine body treatments, facials and nail care and include the use of all spa facilities (sauna, eucalyptus steam room and Jacuzzi).

Paris Gallery Day Spa 02 677 3333

Khalidiya Cantre, Khalidiya, www.uae-parisgallery.com

This spa combines ancient therapies and new technologies in a wide range of treatments. The new menu of chocolate and grape facials and body therapies is a deliciously decadent pampering treatment. Only top quality cocoa powder and essential oils are used to create nourishing and fragrant choc-orange face masks. It's a great way to indulge in your passion for chocolate, without expanding your waistline! The day spa also has a gym with childcare facilities.

Le Spa at Abu Dhabi Ladies' Club 02 666 2228

Al Ras Al Akhdar, www.abudhabiladiesclub.com

You don't have to be a member of the club to enjoy the finest treatments at this relaxing spa. They offer Balinese massage, acupressure and hot stone treatments, as well as an impressive range of facilities including a hydrobath, steam room and three treatment rooms. Keep an eye on the website for their monthly promotions.

Massage

Probably the ultimate way to pamper and unwind is by having a massage. Massage is an area where the multicultural nature of the city comes into play, and you can try an assortment of different types. Available currently are Ayurvedic, Swedish, and Thai massage, which are on offer at various hotels, health clubs and salons in Abu Dhabi. Prices and standards vary, so shop around until you find someone that suits you. The cost for a full body massage ranges from Dhs.100 to 220.

Shopping

Introduction

FROM ENORMOUS MALLS SELLING MODERN MARVELS TO TRADITIONAL SOUKS BRIMMING WITH EXOTIC TREASURES, ABU DHABI'S SHOPPING SCENE IS THE DEFINITION OF VARIETY.

The combination of Abu Dhabi's historical position on many ancient trade routes, and the mix of nationalities passing through the city today, make it a shopping destination of choice for bargain hunters, collectors, souvenir seekers and shopaholics alike. Not only will you find a huge selection of mainstream items, authentic antiques and some unusual discoveries, all at excellent prices, but with shops staying open late into the evenings you can really shop at leisure.

Carpets, gold, spices and wooden antiques are all hot items that find their way into many a homebound tourist's luggage. It's up to you whether you want to spend thousands on a genuine antique or finely woven silk carpet, or whether you want to use your pocket change to buy a few cheap souvenirs. Many stores can make arrangements to ship your purchases back to your home country which is good news if you have blown your baggage allowance!

The size and architecture of Abu Dhabi's malls can be a surprise to some visitors. These huge structures are spacious and fully air-conditioned, and packed with a range of

Shopping

international brands possibly more comprehensive than in your local mall at home. Apart from everyday shops like supermarkets, clothing stores, card shops and electronics outlets, most malls also have several shops selling local souvenirs, carpets and perfume. Malls are much more than just a place to shop, however. Equipped with a range of entertainment and leisure facilities, they are meeting points for families and friends and are busy most of the time.

If you're after a more authentic Arabian shopping experience, head for the traditional markets, or souks. Apart from an eclectic range of goods for sale, the markets are great for an abundance of photo opportunities and a bustling atmosphere that you can see, hear and smell all at once! Items to look out for in the souks include spices, silks, perfumes, souvenirs and antiques. Often shops specialising in certain products can be found side by side, so it's easy to compare prices. If you find a brand name item selling for an unbelievable bargain price, don't believe it. It could be a fake. Souks are usually open from 08:00 to 13:00 and 16:00 to 19:00, except Fridays when they only open in the afternoon.

Bargaining Power

Apart from the amazing atmosphere and exotic goods, souks are also worth visiting to try the traditional way of doing business: bartering through a transaction. Offer the seller half of what he asks, and then bargain your way through the counter-offers. Eventually you'll agree on a mutually satisfactory price. This is not just an accepted way of doing business, it is an *expected* way!

Abu Dhabi's Best Buys

Gold

The UAE is justifiably known as one of the best places in the world to buy gold, and the capital leads the way. Gold in Abu Dhabi is sold according to the fixed daily international gold rate, which is not up for negotiation. However, when buying a piece of jewellery a charge is added for craftmanship and this is where your bargaining power increases. A popular souvenir is to have your name in Arabic made into a gold pendant; most jewellery shops offer this service in white or yellow gold.

There are jewellery shops in most malls, but if you want the best range and more room to bargain, head to either Hamdan Street near the Liwa Centre, or to the Madinat Zayed Gold Centre.

Carpets

Abu Dhabi boasts a huge range of carpets, which are available in various colours, designs, materials and prices. Traditionally, carpets come from Iran, Pakistan, Turkey, China and Central Asia. While salesmen are generally helpful and honest, it helps if you know a little bit about carpets before you agree on a price. As a rough guide, the higher the number of knots per square inch, the higher the price and the better the quality.

Most vendors will happily unroll carpet after carpet, discussing its history and merits at length. Don't feel obliged to purchase just because he has broken a sweat unrolling all his carpets. If you do want to buy, don't forget to stick to your budget and bargain as hard as you can.

Pashminas

Colourful pashminas are widely available. They are great as lightweight shawls (for when the weather is warm but the air conditioning is cold!) and can even be used as winter scarves in cold countries. While genuine pashminas are made from the wool of the pashmina goat (found only in Kashmir, India), most pashminas today are made of a cotton/silk mix, and the ratio dictates the price. Souvenir shops usually have several shelves stacked high with a kaleidoscope of colours. Compare the prices in a few shops to get a feel for quality and price, and have a go at bargaining before you agree on a price.

Other items

Capture the smoothness of a fruity smoke the Middle Eastern way. Shisha pipes are widely available in souvenir shops and hypermarkets, and the tobacco comes in a variety of flavours. Wooden trinket boxes, photo frames and carvings are popular and can be found in souvenir shops. They are often decorated with brass or polished camel bone. The Hamdan Centre has an excellent range of shoes and handbags at bargain prices should you fancy a spree.

Souvenirs

You may find items for sale, such as ivory, which are subject to international trade and import bans or contravene the CITES convention. Don't risk taking them with you. If you wish to buy souvenirs that promote and preserve local handicrafts, and don't break the law, visit Made in UAE (02 644 1575). It sells artwork, photography and gifts and there are branches in the Hilton Abu Dhabi and Cultural Foundation.

Shopping Malls

Abu Dhabi Mall

Tourist Club Area www.abudhabimall.com 02 645 4858

This is one of the main attractions on the Abu Dhabi shopping scene, and a must-visit whether you're looking for a postcard or a Persian carpet. It houses over 200 retail outlets and sees around 26,000 visitors each day. There are restaurants on every floor, a huge multi-screen cinema complex and a children's play area, making it much more than just a shopping destination.

Madinat Zayed Shopping Centre & Gold Centre

Nr Main Post Office, East Road 02 631 8555

With nearly 400 outlets, this mall is a dream for shopaholics. Bargain hunters should head for Daiso, next to the main mall, which is a Japanese store with an eclectic range where most items are Dhs.5. The Madinat Zayed Gold Centre has some of the largest jewellery shops in the Gulf and glitters with the finest gold, diamond and pearl jewellery. The supervised toddler's area and games arcade will keep the kids entertained.

Marina Mall

Breakwater www.marinamall.ae 02 681 8300

Marina Mall claims to be Abu Dhabi's largest. Its beautiful setting on the Breakwater gives it an advantage over other shopping destinations. Home to the capital's branch of IKEA and with more designer boutiques than you could shake a diamond-encrusted stick at, Marina Mall is always busy. It is also home to plenty of restaurants and coffee shops. A snow ski slope, ice rink, and 100 metre viewing tower will all be open soon.

Abu Dhabi Co-operative Society Complex

Shk Zayed St 02 644 0808

This was once home to the Abu Dhabi Co-op (hence the name). Its main draws are now Splash (trendy, inexpensive fashions), Shoe Mart (huge range of shoes), Lifestyle (funky gifts and much more) and The Baby Shop. Other smaller shops include computer suppliers and ladies' fashion outlets.

Fotouh Al Khair Centre

Nr Etisalat Building 02 621 1133

This is home to some of the world's favourite brands including Marks & Spencer and Monsoon. With a host of other outlets selling everything from watches to lingerie and children's fashions, this mall buzzes in the evenings and at the weekends.

Hamdan Centre

Nr Novotel Centre Hotel 02 632 8555

Something of an institution on Abu Dhabi's shopping scene and located in the heart of the city, this vibrant centre is a good place to buy clothing, leather, shoes, sports equipment and touristy knick-knacks, all at reasonable prices. Feel free to practise your bargaining skills here – you'll often get a discount.

Khalifa Centre

Nr Abu Dhabi Coop

This mall, opposite Abu Dhabi Mall (look for Al Mandoos), is teeming with regional craft and souvenir shops, as well as outlets selling Persian and Baluchi carpets. It's an essential stop if you're looking for souvenirs but would rather not visit the souks.

Liwa Centre

Nr Novotel Centre Hotel 02 632 0344

This is where to head on Hamdan Street for jewellery, clothes, makeup, perfume and more. It's a spot where men and women can get glammed up on the cheap. Book lovers should head for House of Prose, an excellent second-hand bookshop. Be sure to visit the vibrant foodcourt on the second level.

Lulu Centre

Al Salam St 02 677 9786

This is an Aladdin's cave selling everything under the sun – from electronics, sportswear and toys, to stationery, clothing, cosmetics and travel accessories. Some items are real bargains, some are pretty tatty, but prices are reasonable.

MultiBrand

Shk Hamdan Street 02 621 9700

This large, open-plan store houses well-known international shops. It's store list sounds like it's come straight from a British high street, with shopes such as Mothercare, Claire's, Next and Oasis. For footwear there's the stylish Milano.

Rotana Mall

Btn Khaleej Al Arab St and Shk Zayed 1st St

Near the corniche, this dinky little mall is best known for a few shops selling antiques, carpets, handicrafts, Arabic pottery and wall hangings. There are some nice pieces here, but see also Made in UAE, on page135.

Al Wahda Mall

Shk Hazza Bin Zayed Street 02 443 7000

With more than 150 shops, a hypermarket and foodcourt, Al Wahda is an impressive addition to Abu Dhabi's retail landscape. The mall covers more than 1.5 million square feet, and features fashion, electronics, jewellery and health and beauty stores across two floors. There is parking for more than 1,500 cars.

Dior
LANCOME
Shopping

Al Ain Mall

Al Ain www.myalainmall.org 03 766 0333

Al Ain Mall has changed the face of shopping in the 'garden city'. With over 100,000 square metres of retail and entertainment space spread over three floors, this bright, modern mall has stores selling a wide range of souvenirs, jewellery and every-day items. The family entertainment area has a 12-lane bowling alley as well as a multi-screen cinema complex and there is an ice-skating rink on the ground floor.

Al Jimi Mall Al Ain

Al Jimi Khabisi
03 763 8883

It may not be the biggest mall in Al Ain (that honour goes to the Al Ain Mall), but Al Jimi is anchored by Carrefour (the French hypermarket chain) and with over 70 stores to choose from there's plenty of shopping to be had there. The mall's extensive range of retail outlets includes Splash, Shoe Mart, Home Centre and the Baby Shop. There's a good selection of food outlets and a large entertainment area to keep the kids busy.

Big Spenders

Thanks to the varied choice of local treasures and shopping pleasures you may find that your purchases exceed your luggage allowance! Luckily, you don't have to curb your shopping spree, as stores are happy to arrange shipments for customers. You will pay by the kilo and rates vary, but you can expect to pay charges of about Dhs. 85 for the UK, Dhs.95 for Australia and Dhs. 180 for the USA.

Souks

THESE TRADITIONAL MARKETS HAVE EVOLVED FROM DUSTY HUBS FOR LIVESTOCK SWAPPING AND BASIC GOODS, INTO BUSTLING TOURIST ATTRACTIONS SELLING A FASCINATING COLLECTION OF ITEMS.

Al Ain Souk

Zayed Bin Sultan St

Also known as the Central or Old Souk, the Al Ain Souk is a great place to explore, savour the local atmosphere, and practise your bargaining skills. The souk itself is a rather ramshackle affair but makes a refreshing change from many of the modern, rather sterile, air-conditioned markets that are appearing elsewhere across the emirates.

Al Ain Camel Market

Nr Town Centre

One of the only camel markets left in the UAE, this is a great way to experience a bit of local trading, while camel blankets make great souvenirs.

Carpet Souk

Al Meena Road

The carpet souk is signposted off the Meena Road. Yemeni mattresses and machine-made carpets dominate, but bargains can be found if you know what you're looking for so

don't forget to haggle. Some of the vendors will make Arabic 'majlis' cushions to order for a very reasonable price. This is also known as the Afghan Souk and it is located on Meena Road near the main port area.

Fish and Fruit & Vegetable Souks

Al Meena

Fish doesn't get much fresher than this! The day's catch is loaded onto the quayside and sold wholesale for the first two hours of trading (04:30 to 06:30), with smaller quantities sold after that. The atmosphere is electric as trading goes on the same way it has for many years. The Fruit & Vegetable Souk across the road is a more relaxed place where an amazing range of produce can be bought by the box or the kilo.

Iranian Souk

Nr Fish Market

It may not be air-conditioned, but this is worth a visit for the fresh batches of Iranian goods which arrive regularly by dhow or barge. Everything is on sale, from household goods and terracotta urns, to decorative metal, cane and glass items.

Mwaifa Souk – Al Ain

Shk Khalifa Bin Zayed St

This modern market consists of a long strip of handy shops, with an intriguing mix of chain stores and independents. There is a bakery, baby shop, toy shop and many more.

Al Zaafaranah Souk

03 762 1868

Al Zaafaranah Souk is one of the largest and most popular in Al Ain. With more than 150 shops – the fruit and vegetable market alone has more than 90 shops – it offers a beguiling range of fresh food, textiles, hand-crafted goods and perfumes. There is also a seafood restaurant and kids' play area.

Keep the Khanjar

If you buy a khanjar (traditional dagger), it will need to be packed in your luggage to go in the hold – even if it's been framed – and you may still need to declare it. If you try to carry it in your hand luggage it will be confiscated.

Going Out

After Hours

VISITORS WILL BE PLEASANTLY SURPRISED AT THE VARIETY OF AFTER-HOURS OPTIONS. WHETHER YOU WANT TO SOAK UP THE ARABIC ATMOSPHERE OR PARTY IN FAMILIAR SURROUNDINGS, THERE'S SOMETHING FOR EVERYONE.

Cosmopolitan and bustling, Abu Dhabi has an excellent and ever-increasing variety of restaurants. From Moroccan to Mexican, Indian to Italian and everything in between, there really is something to suit every palate and budget.

Many of Abu Dhabi's best and most popular restaurants are located in hotels. These are pretty much the only outlets that can serve alcohol with your meal, although some clubs and associations are also permitted to do so. The taxes levied on alcohol translate into fairly high prices for drinks at a restaurant. You will rarely find a bottle of house wine for less than around Dhs.90, and a beer will probably cost you at least Dhs.20 but often more. However, there are quite a number of unlicensed independent restaurants throughout town that are excellent and shouldn't be ignored. In most cases, taxes and service charges are included in menu prices so there won't be any nasty surprises when you get your bill. However, whether these charges are included or not, it should always state this in small print somewhere on the menu. If you want to reward the waiting staff directly then the standard rule of a 10% tip will be appreciated.

Ras Al Akhdar & Breakwater

THERE'S SOMETHING FOR EVERYONE PACKED INTO THE WESTERN TIP OF ABU DHABI. HERE YOU CAN DO IT ALL, FROM INDULGING IN THE SOPHISTICATED LUXURY OF THE EMIRATES PALACE HOTEL TO SAVOURING AN AUTHENTIC MEAL AT ONE OF THE MANY TRADITIONAL RESTAURANTS ON THE BREAKWATER.

1 Al Datrah Restaurant

Emirati

Heritage Village

02 681 4455

Ideally located in the Heritage Village, this traditional cafe is a must. Where else can you stand under a windtower to test the earliest form of air conditioning while you sip on fresh fruit cocktails? You can also marvel at the contrast between the authentic artefacts of a bygone age and the glistening, ultra-modern city across the turquoise waters of the corniche. The menu features typical Arabic fare, with a buffet in the evenings.

2 Gerard Patisserie

Cafe

Marina Mall

02 681 4642

Located at the top of the escalators in this busy mall, Gerard is a great venue for people watching and a quick pitstop during a shopping spree. The simple menu offers light meals such as sandwiches and salads, and of course there is a good selection of pastries and both hot and cold beverages. The service is friendly and efficient.

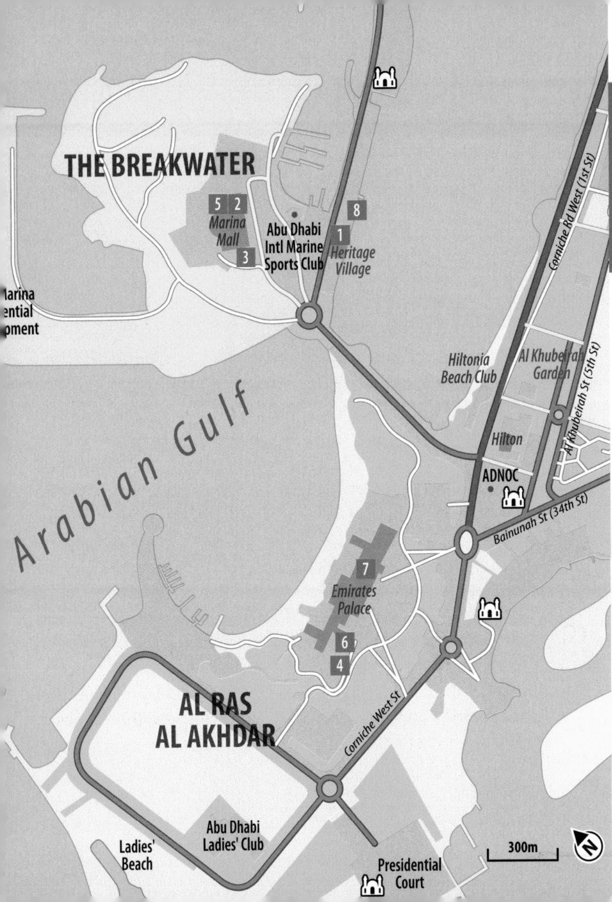

THE BREAKWATER

5 2
Marina Mall
3

Abu Dhabi Intl Marine Sports Club

1
Heritage Village

8

Corniche Rd West (1st St)

...arina
...ential
...pment

Hiltonia Beach Club

Al Khubeirah Garden

Al Khubeirah St (5th St)

Hilton

ADNOC

Arabian Gulf

Bainunah St (34th St)

7
Emirates Palace

6
4

Corniche West St

AL RAS AL AKHDAR

Ladies' Beach

Abu Dhabi Ladies' Club

Presidential Court

300m

N

3 Havana Café

Cafe

Breakwater

02 681 0044

Situated in one of the finest locations in Abu Dhabi, Havana Café has stunning views that encourage relaxed alfresco dining during the cooler months. The international menu has something for everyone, and while breakfast and lunch are fairly quiet affairs, Havana transforms into a vibrant dinner venue as the sun goes down. The service is courteous, and a 'shisha man' in traditional costume is an added attraction.

4 Havana Club

Bar

Emirates Palace

02 690 8021

In keeping with the grandeur of the hotel, the Havana Club exudes opulence and luxury while hinting at the personality of an 'old boys club' type exclusive bar. The bar area has the younger, more outgoing spirit, while the deep leather armchairs tucked in the back are the personification of refinement. Relax and enjoy an exotic cocktail or maybe a vintage brandy, and snack on exquisitely presented canapes. You can even enjoy a fine Cuban cigar or cigarillo. The Havana club is open from 14:00 to 02:00 daily.

5 La Brioche

Cafe

Marina Mall

02 681 5531

The extensive, reasonably priced menu at this charming bistro includes the usual croissants, sandwiches, pizzas and soups, but also has a selection of sweet and savoury crepes, some interesting fruit cocktails and several speciality hot drinks.

6 Mezzaluna

Italian

Emirates Palace

02 690 7070

From the time the complimentary breads and olives are placed in front of you, until the time you devour the last crumb of your wicked (but wonderful) dessert, your experience at Mezzaluna will be a guaranteed delight. The Italian head chef uses divine inspiration to create a host of beautifully presented dishes, including fresh pasta concoctions, seafood creations and meat dishes, many of which are surprisingly easy on the pocket. Stunning decor and an opulent atmosphere also please.

7 Sayad

Seafood

Emirates Palace

02 690 7033

As the flagship restaurant of the luxurious Emirates Palace Hotel, you can expect the ultimate dining experience. This superb restaurant offers a seasonal menu of fresh seafood from across the globe. Select your own fish or lobster from the tanks along the wall, and it will be prepared to your exact tastes, or opt for the five-course set menu which will give you a taste of everything from sushi to the catch of the day. Luxury touches like a cooling towel spritzed with jasmine adds to the elegance and sophistication. A simply sublime dining option!

8 Shuja Yacht

Dinner Cruise

Opp Marina Mall

02 695 0551

A two-hour cruise aboard this sleek vessel is a unique way to celebrate in style, have an intimate evening or socialise in a large group. Food is served buffet style, with lobster tails, prawns and crabs vying for a place on your plate along with lamb, chicken and a myriad of side dishes.

Corniche West

SOME OF ABU DHABI'S MOST POPULAR INTERNATIONAL RESTAURANTS AND NIGHTSPOTS ARE FOUND AT THE HILTON AND INTERCONTINENTAL HOTELS. TO MAKE THE EXPERIENCE UNIQUE, UNLEASH YOUR CREATIVITY AT CAFE CERAMIQUE WHERE YOU CAN PAINT YOUR CROCKERY, AS WELL AS DRINK OUT OF IT!

1 Al Mawal

Arabic

Hilton Abu Dhabi — 02 681 1900

After showing you to your table, the welcoming and attentive staff swiftly serve you with complimentary baskets of fresh vegetables, bread, olives and more, and the exhaustive menu covers even the most exclusive dishes. Live entertainment comprising a band, a belly dancer and a singer completes the experience. Although a it is a bit pricey, this restaurant is worth every dirham.

2 BiCE

Italian

Hilton Abu Dhabi — 02 681 1900

For modern Italian cooking with a touch of romance, BiCE is a good choice. Low lighting and flickering candles on every table provide an intimate atmosphere while the decor is relaxed elegance. The hand-made pasta, and a good range of seafood dishes, are all prepared with care and presented with a flourish. It's Italian but with a twist on the traditional recipes – spaghetti with lobster bolognaise.

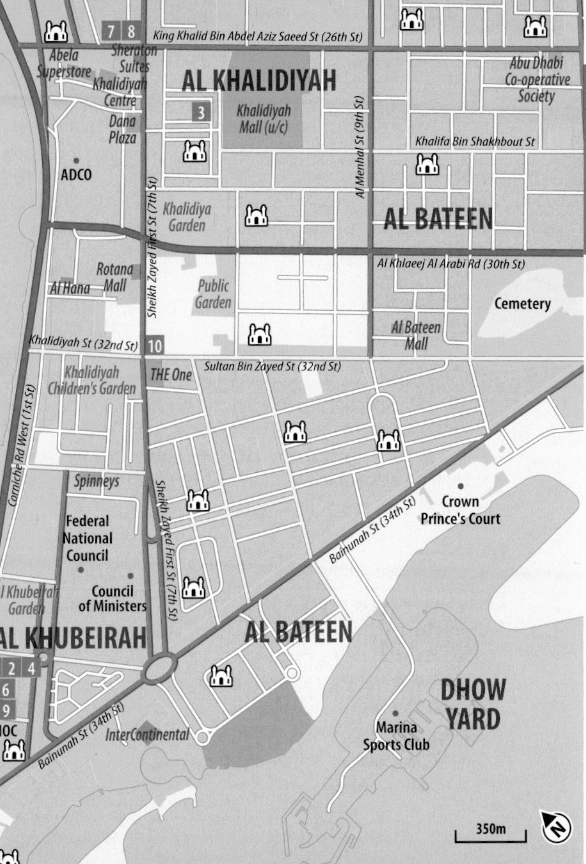
King Khalid Bin Abdel Aziz Saeed St (26th St)
Abela Superstore
Sheraton Suites
Khalidiyah Centre
Dana Plaza
AL KHALIDIYAH
Khalidiyah Mall (u/c)
Abu Dhabi Co-operative Society
Al Menhal St (9th St)
Khalifa Bin Shakhbout St
ADCO
Khalidiya Garden
AL BATEEN
Sheikh Zayed First St (7th St)
Al Khlaeej Al Arabi Rd (30th St)
Rotana Mall
Al Hana
Public Garden
Cemetery
Al Bateen Mall
Khalidiyah St (32nd St)
Sultan Bin Zayed St (32nd St)
Khalidiyah Children's Garden
THE One
Corniche Rd West (1st St)
Spinneys
Sheikh Zayed First St (7th St)
Crown Prince's Court
Bainunah St (34th St)
Federal National Council
Council of Ministers
Al Khubeirah Garden
AL KHUBEIRAH
AL BATEEN
DHOW YARD
ADNOC
Bainunah St (34th St)
InterContinental
Marina Sports Club
350m

3 Café Ceramique Abu Dhabi — Cafe

Nr Choithram, Khalidiya — 02 666 4412

The novelty factor is high at Café Ceramique, with its trendy layout, 'naked' ceramics and arty magazines – definitely a good place to go if you want to develop your inner artist! While you work on creating your next masterpiece, you can munch on a variety of light meals and snacks. The food is innovatively presented and tasty.

4 Coconut Bay — Mongolian

Hiltonia Beach Club — 02 681 1900

The a la carte menu at Coconut Bay is impressive, but during the cooler months the Mongolian barbecue on Friday evenings is a hands-down winner. The extensive selection of sandwiches and the original salads make this a great place to recharge after a hard day's relaxing on the beach – the setting is ideal for a casual dinner and a few sundowners. There's also a special kids' menu that's sure to please.

5 Idioms — Cafe

Corniche Road West — 02 681 0808

This trendy yet unpretentious 'new kid on the block' has an interesting menu, friendly staff and a good location (near the corniche in Khalidiya). The menu includes salads, sandwiches and some rather tasty pastas and main dishes. The signature espresso cocktails served in shot glasses – a 'sweet swiss' or a 'sweet afro' – adds a unique finish to a pleasant dining experience, and shouldn't be missed.

6 Jazz Bar & Dining

Bar

Hilton Abu Dhabi

02 681 1900

For a relaxed evening of jazz, champagne and good food in a stylish setting, the Jazz Bar is worth a visit. Each dish on the extensive menu is available in two sizes – 'down beat' for the not so hungry, and 'main melody' for the ravenous. Special dietary needs can be met on request. As can be expected in any good bar, the wine list and drinks selection are impressive. The popular band 'Southern Glow' keeps the rhythm alive and attracts a crowd, especially on weekends.

7 La Veranda

Buffet

Sheraton Suites Abu Dhabi

02 666 6220

An upscale hotel restaurant with daily theme nights and good quality buffet fare to tempt everyone. It is a challenge to leave this restaurant feeling hungry as there is something delicious to suit all tastes. The dessert table is especially enticing so make sure you leave room. The decor is stylish and upmarket, and the service friendly and attentive.

8 Lebanese Flower

Arabic

Nr Choithram, Khalidiya

02 666 6888

This popular restauant has a range of high quality grilled meats and fish accompanied by delicious freshly baked Arabic bread. A selection of Middle Eastern curries and meat dishes is available at lunchtime. Service is super efficient – the slightest nod of your head will instantly bring a bevy of enthusiastic waiters to your table.

9 Tequilana Discotheque

Club

Hilton Abu Dhabi

02 681 1900

Transport yourself to a tropical beach, dotted with thatched huts and palm trees glistening under a starry night sky at this cleverly decorated, upmarket discotheque inside the Hemingways complex. The resident DJ gets the crowd jumping with a mix of fresh sounds and if you're an exhibitionist at heart the semi-private karaoke room is where you'll find like minded souls. Salsa nights and regular promotions usually bring in the crowds.

10 THE One

Cafe

Shk Zayed 1st St

02 681 6500

With soft lighting and smart furnishings, this cafe echoes the shop in which it's situated. There are three distinct menus depending on your mood: the 'Chic' menu is crammed with healthy options, 'Vogue' features traditional dishes including soups and salads, and 'Risque' is home to familiar dishes with an unexpected twist, such as Mexican falafel. Vegetarians will be particularly pleased with the selection on offer.

11 Vasco's

Bar

Hiltonia Beach Club

02 692 4328

Vasco's is a contemporary, fine dining venue offering a fusion of European, Arabic and Asian cuisines. Food is prepared to a very high standard and imaginatively presented. The patio offers a pleasant, alfresco setting, and as this is one of the more popular restaurants in Abu Dhabi, reservations are recommended whether for lunch and dinner.

WHETHER YOU ARE LOOKING FOR FINE DINING, AUTHENTIC INDIAN CUISINE, OR A UNIQUE PERSPECTIVE FROM THE CAPITAL'S ONLY REVOLVING RESTAURANT, THIS IS THE PLACE TO BE. AND AFTER A FINE MEAL YOU CAN END THE EVENING OFF BY JOINING THE LOCALS IN A STROLL ALONG THE CORNICHE.

1 Al Aris Restaurant & Grill

Arabic

Al Salam St

02 645 5503

Al Aris is one of the many clean and cheerful Arabic/Lebanese restaurants conveniently located on Salam Street. Standard fare (not forgetting the classic shawarma) is served by efficient and friendly staff, making this an ideal spot for a quick meal or takeaway. The fruit juices are incredibly fresh and the prices are reasonable. Seating is available outside as well as inside with a family room on the upper level.

2 Amalfi

Italian

Le Royal Meridien Hotel

02 674 2020

For a taste of authentic Italy, Amalfi offers fresh pasta, risotto and seafood cooked to perfection by a Sicilian chef. The chic, Italian-inspired design (think Milan and the fashionistas), is open and airy, with big windows overlooking the terrace and pool. Traditional Italian music from the Sonata Duonello provides an excellent background to this stunning restaurant. The feel is unfussy, uncomplicated, and simple elegance, lending itself to intimacy and romance.

Corniche Hospital
14
Al Diar Dana
7 8 12
Al Diar Mina
International Rotana Inn
16 Al Diar Regency
Sheraton
TOURIST CLUB AREA
1
Electra St
15 Lulu Centre
13
3
Al Salam St (8th St)
Hamdan Bin Mohamed St (5th St)
Sheikh Zayed First St (7th St)
9th St
Al Ain Palace
2
Le Royal Meridien
Diplomatic
4 5
21 22 24 25
Zakher
Millennium
Grand Continental
Dr. McCulloch's Clinic
Al Diar Sands
20
6 19
Bani Yas St (6th St)
Corniche Rd East
Crown Plaza
9 11
10
Khalifa Bin Zayed St (3rd St)
Bhs 18
Al Falah St (9th St)
26
Corniche Residence Hilton
Hamdan Centre
Lulu St (4th St)
Al Noor Hospital
17 23
Al Sharqi St (4th St)
AL DHAFRAH
MARKAZIYAH
Novotel Centre
Madinat Zayed
Gold Souk
Al Falah Plaza
Liwa Centre
Central Post Office
trOleum hibition
Liwa St
New Souk
Central Market (u/c)
Al Diar Palm
New Medical Centre
MADINAT ZAYED
Sheikh Rashid Bin Saeed Al Maktoum St (2nd St)
mber mmerce
Fish Market & Vegetable Souk
Cultural Foundation
21
Qasr Al Hosn
Al Muhairy Centre
Khalid Bin Waleed St (22nd St)
Grand Stores
Central Hospital
Corniche Rd West
Bainunah Hilton Tower
Al Manhal Palace
Sheikh Khalifa Medical City
Tariq Bin Zayed St
Al Manhal St (9th St)
AL HOSN
AL MANHAL
AL ZAAB
Al Markaziyah Garden
Al Hosn Plaza
Sheikh Zayed First St (7th St)
Agriculture Research Laboratory
350m
N

3 Caravan

Asian

Hamed Centre

02 639 3370

For a cheap, no-frills Asian meal, Caravan certainly delivers the goods. The menu offers a tasty selection of Chinese, Indian and Thai cuisine, and the great value for money evening buffet includes soups, salads, a selection of main courses and desserts. The service is remarkably friendly and helpful given that this is a low-cost venue.

4 Casa Goa

Indian

Zakher Hotel

02 627 7701

Casa Goa may appear a bit rough around the edges, but if you're the kind of person that eats raw chillies for fun you'll love their range of mouth-melting curries. A warning to the uninitiated – south Indian cuisine is far spicier than the milder northern dishes, but thankfully this venue is licensed so you can douse the flames with a frosty beer. If you like dining somewhat off the beaten track then check out Casa Goa.

5 Chili's

Tex-Mex

Grand Al Mariah Cineplex

02 671 6300

It's not just the food that will attract you to Chili's. The enticing Tex-Mex menu brimming with juicy steaks, spicy chicken and lots of cheese and refried beans is certainly reason enough to go, and the super helpful service and family friendly atmosphere keeps punters coming back. Prices may seem high for a casual family restaurant, but the quality is superb. 'Guilt free' menu options will please the health conscious.

6 Cristal Cigar & Champagne Bar

Millennium Hotel

Cigar Bar

02 626 2700

Once the masterful bar manager has poured you a glass of champagne and helped you select the perfect smoke, you can sit back and relax in surroundings of polished wood, leather and subdued lighting. The tinkling tunes played by the in-house pianist make the perfect accompaniment, and if all this sophistication leaves you feeling peckish, a small range of tasty snacks is available.

7 Cloud Nine - Cigar & Bottle Club — Bar

Sheraton Abu Dhabi Resort & Towers — 02 677 3333

From the first puff on your hand-picked Cohiba, Monte Cristo or Bolivar (delivered to you on a silver platter), to the last bit of Beluga passing your lips, this luxurious venue exudes a pleasing mix of old boys' charm and trendy sophistication. Service is pleasant and discreet, and a pianist adds further elegance to a classy (albeit smoky) evening out.

8 El Sombrero — Tex-Mex

Sheraton Abu Dhabi Resort & Towers — 02 677 3333

Whether you're out for a relaxed dinner for two or a raucous night with your amigos, El Sombrero comes highly recommended. Fascinating Mexican artefacts and well thought out decor set the scene, while the food and the service both score highly. This lively venue is good on any night of the week but particularly worth checking out are the theme nights on Tuesdays and Wednesdays.

9 The Garden — International

Crowne Plaza — 02 621 0000

This faux alfresco 'garden' venue is decorated with an abundance of plants and even has a waterfall. Theme nights cover the cuisines of the world, and every evening you'll find an impressive buffet designed to delight your taste buds. The Friday brunch is a popular family affair, with truckloads of tasty food and plenty of entertainment for the kids, so you can enjoy a long lunch with a variety of liquid refreshments!

10 Harvesters Pub

Pub

Al Diar Sands Hotel

02 633 5335

This smoky basement bar has the atmosphere of a traditional British pub, with live entertainment and four busy dartboards. Accordingly, the menu offers traditional English 'cuisine', such as all-day breakfast, bangers and mash, and even chip butties. This lively bar is usually heaving with a predominantly male expat crowd, no doubt recalling fond memories of their local pubs back home.

11 Heroes Diner

American

Crowne Plaza

02 621 0000

Arguably the city's best sports bar, Heroes is nearly always heaving with frenzied fans that come to watch the game in the company of similarly sports-mad folk. The familiar pub fare is tasty and portions are generous. Thankfully the table service is friendly and surprisingly efficient, so there is no need to wrestle your way through the crowds just to get to the bar. Regular events such as Ladies Night, Quiz Night and Dance Night pack even more punters in.

12 Il Paradiso

Seafood

Sheraton Abu Dhabi Resort & Towers

02 677 3333

Offering one of the capital's most scenic outdoor dining experiences, this is a leading player in Abu Dhabi's competitive seafood scene. Seafood lovers will not be disappointed by the range of fish and shellfish, all of which are imaginatively presented. It's not cheap (watch out for the 'cooking charge'), but the food is good and the service friendly and efficient.

13 India Palace

Indian

Opp ADNOC, Al Salam St

02 644 8777

This unassuming restaurant features an extensive menu and is generally busy. The food is tasty and at times pretty fiery, and portions are generous offering good value for your dirham. Those with more delicate palates can request milder versions of their favourites. Quick, courteous waiters will patiently guide you through the menu if you are not an expert on North Indian Cuisine.

14 Jade

Far Eastern

Al Diar Mina Hotel

02 678 1000

Enter the stark minimalism of the Jade interior for a lighter, healthier twist on Far Eastern cuisine – think fusion rather than authentic Japanese or Chinese. The appetisers, including chicken dumplings, sushi and sashimi, are good value for money and are light enough to pave the way for a main course dish such as black bean noodles or teriyaki smoked salmon. The small selection of conventional wines should steer you towards the Japanese sake, served hot or cold.

15 Kwality

Indian

Opp Blue Marine, Al Salam St

02 672 7337

If you like authentic Indian food at a very reasonable price, then Kwality is one of the best options in town. From North Indian Tandoori dishes to Goan curries, Kwality provides a wonderful tour through Indian cuisine. The food, service, and welcoming atmosphere make this one of the 'must do' Indian restaurants in the capital.

16 La Mamma

Italian

Sheraton Abu Dhabi Resort & Towers

02 677 3333

This spacious, well-appointed restaurant is an excellent choice for a romantic evening, a fun family feast or a respectable business meal. With the exception of the exotic antipasto buffet, the food is fairly standard but is well prepared and of good quality, from quick and filling pizzas to delicious and generous helpings of pasta and seafood.

17 Le Beaujolais

French

Novotel Centre Hotel

02 633 3555

With its red-checked tablecloths and French-speaking, glass-clinking clientele, Le Beaujolais virtually transports you to a charming little bistro in Paris. The menu offers seafood and meat dishes, rounded off with a dessert selection including crackly crusted crème brulee. A daily set menu is also available. The service, headed by a friendly maitre d', is welcoming and attentive, but never obtrusive.

18 Le Boulanger

Cafe

Bhs Building, Shk Hamdan Bin Mohd. St

02 631 8115

This busy French cafe in the heart of the city is a great place to enjoy a European style breakfast, good coffee and a browse through the daily newspapers from around the world. The menu is extensive, featuring tasty food in generous quantities. There is a bakery counter selling the freshest breads, croissants, tarts and cakes, which can be eaten on the premises or taken home to enjoy later (or both!).

19 Marakesh

Moroccan

Millennium Hotel

02 626 2700

Despite its elaborate decor, Marakesh has a fairly casual ambience where exotic and delectable Moroccan food (with more than a hint of Lebanese influence) is served in generous portions by highly efficient waiters. A live band adds atmosphere, and later in the evening an eye-poppingly beautiful belly dancer makes a dramatic appearance.

20 Nihal Restaurant

Indian

Nr Sands Htl, Shk Zayed 2nd St

02 631 8088

This established Indian restaurant offers great curries at rock bottom prices, and the menu is extensive enough to tickle just about anyone's fancy. The fragrant spices of the subcontinent are all expertly blended into tasty traditional dishes, served up with the usual relishes, yoghurts and chutneys. If Indian food is not your favourite, there are also various Chinese dishes on offer. Nihal does a bustling takeaway trade too.

21 Panda Panda Chinese Restaurant — Chinese

Nr Jashanmal, Al Istiqlal St — 02 633 9300

This contemporary eatery mixes modern and traditional oriental influences. The extensive menu caters equally well to vegetarians, seafood lovers and carnivores, with the hot and sour soup and the Schezuan beef both heartily recommended. Service is quick, attentive and enthusiastic, and if the prices seem a little high, remember that portions are usually generous enough to feed two.

22 P.J.O'Reillys — Pub

Le Royal Meridien Hotel — 02 674 2020

This Irish pub is extremely popular, with a friendly and inviting atmosphere. The menu is pub grub with flair, with large portions and good value for money. The lively bar downstairs is the place to meet and greet, though you can escape to the quieter upstairs or alfresco dining areas. Big-screen TVs show sport, though the sound is generally only on during live football matches. Happy Hour runs from 12:00 to 20:00 every day, with other specials happening regularly through the week.

23 Restaurant China — Chinese

Novotel Centre Hotel — 02 633 3555

This restaurant has been dishing up yummy Chinese cuisine to its satisfied customers for over 20 years now, and it's still going strong. The food and service are both of consistently high standards, with the Peking duck and kung pao prawns worthy of a special mention. The authentic decor and directional lighting enhance the warm, welcoming ambience.

24 SAX
Bar

Le Royal Meridien Hotel
02 674 2020

Yuppies and the chic set will love this restaurant with its vibrant, trendy, New York style. A live jazz band and a well-stocked bar contribute to the vibey atmosphere as you unwind on the comfortable sofas in the sunken lounge area, with one of the many exotic cocktails on offer. Like most trendy eateries, the quality of the ingredients and presentation cannot be faulted, and special drink offers and free cocktails for the ladies help to make the evening even more enjoyable.

25 Soba
Japanese

Le Royal Meridien Hotel
02 674 2020

Although sushi is not everyone's choice, bypassing this restaurant means missing out on a delightful culinary experience. The food is beautifully presented and delicious, and for non-sushi eaters there are a number of alternatives. Waiters are on hand to make helpful suggestions and the chefs are in plain sight, making intriguing viewing. The decor is minimalist and the seating does not encourage lingering.

26 Zyara Café
Cafe

Next to Corniche Residence
02 627 5006

Zyara in Arabic means 'visit,' and this trendy cafe definitely deserves one. The glass frontage offers a good view of the corniche, and the laidback interior, with its rustic, Victorian style is an ideal meeting place. The quality and presentation of the food is excellent and the service is friendly and attentive, but all this does come at a price.

Al Meena & Tourist Club Area

CHOOSE FROM A DINNER CRUISE ON A TRADITIONAL DHOW FROM AL MEENA PORT OR SOME OF ABU DHABI'S FAVOURITE RESTAURANTS IN THE TOURIST CLUB AREA. EITHER WAY YOU WILL HAVE A MEMORABLE EVENING WITH EXCELLENT FOOD AND PLENTY OF PHOTO OPS.

1 Al Areesh

Emirati

Al Dhafra

02 673 2266

For an authentic Arabian experience, look no further. At Al Areesh, guests are instantly welcomed and assisted in choosing from a buffet comprising an attractive selection of seafood, chicken and meat. Food at this restaurant is extremely fresh and plentiful. A healthy choice of 'local' and traditional starters, mains and desserts can be washed down with freshly made fruit cocktails that are highly recommended. This is definitely a hidden gem.

2 The Alamo

Tex-Mex

Abu Dhabi Marina

02 644 0300

This restaurant, with its cantina style atmosphere and typical Alamo memorabilia, is renowned for its frozen margaritas, succulent spare ribs and sizzling fajitas. An 'All You Can Eat' menu inclusive of unlimited house beverages is available Friday to Tuesday from 19:00 to 23:00. Friendly and polite staff and an entertaining Latino band complete the ingredients for a great fun night out.

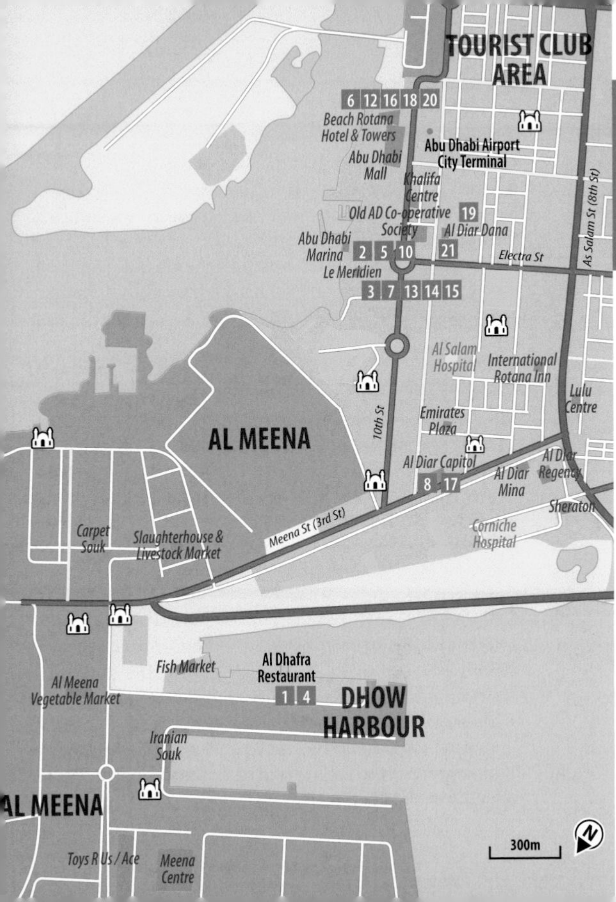

TOURIST CLUB AREA
6 12 16 18 20
Beach Rotana Hotel & Towers
Abu Dhabi Airport City Terminal
Abu Dhabi Mall
Khalifa Centre
Old AD Co-operative Society
19
Al Diar Dana
Abu Dhabi Marina
2 5 10
21
Electra St
As Salam St (8th St)
Le Meridien
3 7 13 14 15
Al Salam Hospital
International Rotana Inn
Lulu Centre
10th St
Emirates Plaza
AL MEENA
Al Diar Capitol
Al Diar Regency
8 17
Al Diar Mina
Sheraton
Meena St (3rd St)
Corniche Hospital
Carpet Souk
Slaughterhouse & Livestock Market
Fish Market
Al Dhafra Restaurant
Al Meena Vegetable Market
1 4
DHOW HARBOUR
Iranian Souk
AL MEENA
Toys R Us / Ace
Meena Centre
300m
N

3 Al Birkeh

Arabic

Le Meridien Abu Dhabi — 02 644 6666

Widely touted as one of the best Arabic restaurants in town, this established venue serves traditional Middle Eastern fare in a festive setting, complete with live music and a belly dancer. Start your culinary journey with a selection of hot and cold mezze before moving on to your main course of grilled meat or fish (and lots of it!). For the gastronomically brave only, the menu includes some exotic dishes such as raw liver, washed down with the strong aniseed drink 'arak'.

4 Al Dhafra

Dinner Cruise

Nr Fish Market, Al Meena Dhow Harbour — 02 673 2266

This traditional dhow offers daily dinner cruises along the picturesque corniche. The upper deck boasts a majlis and the lower air-conditioned deck can seat approximately 50 people. A sumptuous menu includes lavish Arabic fare, and as you dine, the ethnic charm of the dhow and the serenity of the placid Arabian waters will ensure an unforgettable evening.

5 Bam Bu!

Chinese

Abu Dhabi Marina — 02 645 6373

Whether out for a romantic meal or a group dinner, you can't go wrong with Bam Bu! – a little slice of the Orient with an enchanting view of the yachts at the Marina. The set menu (Dhs.99, including unlimited selected beverages) is a good choice for the uninitiated – just sit back and relax while a constant stream of freshly prepared delicacies are brought to your table.

6 Benihana

Japanese

Beach Rotana Hotel & Towers,

02 644 3000

The gracious, contemporary Japanese cuisine, the minimalist decor and the crowd-pleasing teppanyaki chefs make this venue a must. The menu includes the usual soups, salads and desserts, but if it's Japanese you're after then don't miss out on the sushi and of course the teppanyaki, prepared at live cooking stations by entertaining chefs. Prices may seem high but for a feast of melt-in-your-mouth treats, it's good value.

7 Captain's Arms

Pub

Le Meridien Abu Dhabi

02 644 6666

Overlooking the gardens and located in the Culinary Village, this tavern, with its cosy interior and upbeat, outdoor terrace, offers the ambience of a traditional British pub. The daily happy hour (17:00 – 20:00), nightly entertainment, and food and drink specials bring in the crowds. Food portions are generous and generally satisfying, although you won't find many culinary surprises here.

8 Ciro's Pomodoro

Italian

Al Diar Capital Hotel

02 678 7700

If you just can't resist a charming Italian, then this venue is perfect for you. The menu covers all the classics like pastas, salads, pizzas and grilled dishes, and the numerous pictures of celebrities visiting Ciro's around the world will keep you entertained. The food is delectable, the service friendly, and most evenings there's a live band to serenade you through your meal.

9 The Club Restaurant

International

The Club

02 673 1111

The softly lit, Roman-style interior is the perfect setting for a romantic evening. With its regular theme nights, The Club Restaurant offers a superb choice of different cuisines, each as tasty as the next. The service is attentive and the prices reasonable. Reservations are required but make sure you and your date arrive together as mobile phones are banned!

10 Colosseum
Nightclub
Abu Dhabi Marina
02 644 0300

Visit this Roman-style nightclub any night of the week and rub shoulders with the young and hip on the snug, yet pumping, dance floor. The latest R&B and pop fusion beats, belted out by capable DJs, make this multicultural venue one of the city's favourite hotspots. As an added bonus, drinks are reasonably priced and ladies get in free.

11 Dilmah T-Bar
Cafe
The Club
02 673 1111

T-Bar is a haven for tea connoisseurs, with an exhaustive selection of teas to choose from and deep, comfy sofas to sink into while you sip on your favourite cuppa. Each cup of tea is accompanied by a mouthwatering homemade cookie, and there are newspapers and magazines to read, should your company be a little tedious.

12 L.A.B.
Bar
Beach Rotana Hotel & Towers
02 644 3000

Before 22:00, this is a sophisticated meeting place for those who want to chat. Arrive later if you'd rather party in a cross between a futuristic, all flashing nightspot and an Ibiza rave. In contrast to the loud but attractively lit bar area, the spacious terrace overlooking the beach is relaxed and welcoming. Not the cheapest drinking hole in town but certainly a stylish venue with potential for a good time. Don't be deceived by the refreshing taste of the cocktails as they're strong.

13 Le Bistro

French

Le Meridien Abu Dhabi

02 644 6666

Connoisseurs of fine wines and elegant French cuisine will enjoy a superb culinary experience at Le Bistro in Le Meridien's central garden. In cooler months, the terrace offers a great opportunity to watch the world go by while feasting on some top quality fare. The menu is a little limited but fans of simple fish and meat dishes prepared in a classic French style will be more than happy. Cheap it ain't, but you get what you pay for.

14 Maharaja

Indian

Le Meridien Abu Dhabi

02 644 6666

There's certainly no shortage of excellent Indian food in the capital, but this venue provides a five-star setting and impeccable service to go with it. The decor is carefully thought out, from the crisp table linen to the interesting knick-knacks on the walls. The food is tasty and expertly prepared, and although the bias is towards northern cuisine, the chef often creates dishes from other regions. The Thursday buffet lets you sample a bit of everything at a reasonable price.

15 Pappagallo

Italian

Le Meridien Abu Dhabi

02 644 6666

Pappagallo is like a little slice of Tuscany right in the heart of the Le Meridien Culinary Village. The menu caters to most tastes, offering all the usual favourites of Italian cuisine, such as pastas and pizzas, as well as a wonderful antipasto buffet. Whether you dine alfresco or indoors, the food is good, the atmosphere pleasant, and the service satisfactory.

16 Prego's

Italian

Beach Rotana Hotel & Towers — 02 644 3000

Prego's boasts a large, airy interior and superb terrace overlooking the beach. The food is wonderful – in addition to the pizzas prepared in an authentic wood-fired oven, the menu has a selection of both classic and innovative pasta dishes, main courses and desserts. The venue is family friendly, but the comfortable spaces between tables make this a good choice for an intimate dinner too.

17 Rock Bottom Café

American

Al Diar Capital Hotel — 02 677 7655

Named after the Wall Street crash, this vibrant American diner has a somewhat split personality – go early in the evening to enjoy a quiet dinner, or hang around until later when the live music starts and the pace becomes frenetic. The menu features succulent steaks, sizzling seafood and innovative salads, as well as a range of lighter snacks.

18 Rodeo Grill

Steakhouse

Beach Rotana Hotel & Towers — 02 644 3000

Enter the hallowed 'gentlemen's club' atmosphere of this premium steakhouse and you won't regret it – the food is of particularly high quality, the venue is sublime and the service faultless. Steak lovers will be especially pleased by the first-class selection of Angus, Australian, tenderloin, ribeye and bison steaks, while a range of seafood and poultry alternatives is also available.

19 Riviera

Arabic

Tourist Club Area

02 676 6615

This bright and airy cafe mixes a relaxed Mediterranean setting with typical Lebanese cuisine. The tasty mezze and freshly grilled dishes are recommended, and accompanied perfectly by piping hot Arabic bread, which is baked on the premises. You'll even find a few European specialities on the menu, just in case Lebanese food doesn't tickle your fancy.

20 Trader Vic's

Polynesian

Beach Rotana Hotel & Towers

02 644 3000

Whether for business or pleasure, Trader Vic's is one of Abu Dhabi's long-standing favourite restaurants. The consistent quality of the food, the attentive staff and the relaxed tropical ambience keep people coming back time and time again. Try one of their world-famous cocktails as you peruse the exciting menu of tantalising French Polynesian dishes.

21 49er's The Gold Rush

American

Al Diar Dana Hotel

02 645 6000

Centrally situated, this popular venue is often packed so get there early to enjoy an entire evening of entertainment. The rich timber finishes reflect a traditional ranch-type atmosphere, and the food is delicious, with steaks that melt in the mouth. Service cannot be faulted, and with live music and reasonable prices you can't go too wrong.

Al Ain

AL AIN MAY HAVE A RELAXED AMBIENCE BUT THERE ARE PLENTY OF DINING OPTIONS HERE, WHETHER YOU'RE LOOKING FOR INTERNATIONAL CUISINE OR TRADITIONAL ARABIC FARE. FOR THE MOST STUNNING VIEW THE MERCURE GRAND HOTEL ATOP JEBEL HAFEET IS A MUST.

1 Al Khayam

Persian

Hilton Al Ain

03 768 6666

The authentic Persian surroundings alone justify a reservation. An extensive and varied wine list caters for all tastes and complements an array of Iranian grills, kebabs and other Middle Eastern delights. The delicious fresh bread and tangy salads add to the other dining pleasures and table service is prompt and cheerful.

2 Arabesque

International

Al Ain InterContinental Hotel

03 768 6686

This top hotel buffet comes at a very affordable price. Served in spacious, attractive surroundings by polite and unobtrusive staff, the meal includes salads that are fresh and varied, and plenty of alternatives to the ubiquitous Lebanese mezze. Hot dishes are well prepared and presented, covering a wide range of tastes and geographic backgrounds. Lunch is spiced up with a live cooking centre featuring a cuisine of the day and evenings include a small set menu that complements the buffet. And the desserts are definitely worth the drive.

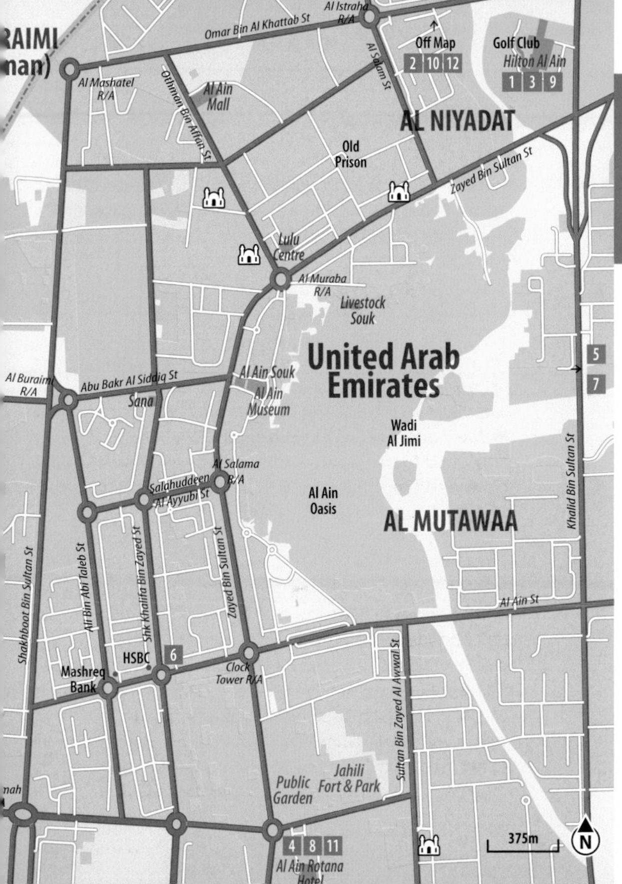
AIMI
nan)
Omar Bin Al Khattab St
Al Istraha R/A
Al Mashatel R/A
Othman Bin Affan St
Al Ain Mall
Al Salam St
Off Map
2 10 12
Golf Club
Hilton Al Ain
1 3 9
AL NIYADAT
Old Prison
Zayed Bin Sultan St
Lulu Centre
Al Muraba R/A
Livestock Souk
United Arab Emirates
Al Buraimi R/A
Abu Bakr Al Siddiq St
Sana
Al Ain Souk
Al Ain Museum
5
7
Wadi Al Jimi
Khalid Bin Sultan St
Al Salama R/A
Salahuddeen Al Ayyubi St
Al Ain Oasis
AL MUTAWAA
Ali Bin Abi Taleb St
Shk Khalifa Bin Zayed St
Zayed Bin Sultan St
Shakhboot Bin Sultan St
Al Ain St
HSBC
6
Mashreq Bank
Clock Tower R/A
Sultan Bin Zayed Al Awwal St
Jahili Fort & Park
Public Garden
nah
4 8 11
Al Ain Rotana Hotel
375m
N

3 Casa Romana

Italian

Hilton Al Ain

03 768 6666

The well-known Casa Romana, overlooking the bustling lobby of the hotel, has an extensive menu of authentic Italian dishes, all generously portioned and delicious. Expect to find all your Italian favourites here, including pizza, pasta and a rather tasty seafood risotto. The decor evokes the feel of a rustic country terrace.

4 Gardinia

Mediterranean

Al Ain Rotana Hotel

03 751 5111

Live piano music fills the air while a carved ice swan presides over an array of fresh seafood laid out in a wooden dhow – welcome to Gardinia. This venue is popular throughout the week and reservations are a necessity. Seafood lovers won't know where to start but the seafood chowder is recommended and the red snapper is a treat. As for the desserts, if you have room then you won't be disappointed.

5 Eden Rock

Arabic

Mercure Grand Jebel Hafeet

03 783 8888

Location is everything (or so estate agents say) and the half-hour drive up Jebel Hafeet mountain for a spectacular view, and temperatures six to eight degrees cooler, make this well worth the trip. Sit on the terrace at night to get a dramatic sense of place, sample a standard Arabic buffet until 22:00 and carry on with a shisha until 02:00, while taking in a 180° vista of the Al Ain lights twinkling below.

6 The Hut

Cafe

Nr Pizza Hut, Khalifa St — 03 751 6526

If you long for the charm of the cafes of Europe, you may have found your home from home here. It offers an oasis of calm on the bustling Khalifa Street, with its warmly decorated interior and gentle ambience. Recommended for breakfasts and all-day snacks, the food is consistently pleasant and servings are generous.

7 Le Belvedere

International

Mercure Grand Jebel Hafeet — 03 783 8888

Perched atop Jebel Hafeet, Le Belvedere has a wonderful (yet restricted) view over the city of Al Ain. Serving both buffet and a la carte meals, this restaurant offers a variety of international cuisine with a distinct Mediterranean influence. The Friday seafood buffet is a speciality and well worth the drive to the top of the mountain. But perhaps the best way to experience Le Belvedere is to book in for a night at the hotel, and enjoy the full package.

8 Min Zaman

Arabic

Al Ain Rotana Hotel, — 03 754 5111

Once you manage to find this restaurant in the depths of the Rotana hotel (ask for directions at reception), you are in for a superb evening of regional food and entertainment. Hot and cold mezze head the menu, followed by the usual grilled meats and fish, while desserts and shisha are all enjoyed against a backdrop of live music, singing and belly dancing. It gets crowded on Thursday nights, so reservations are recommended.

9 Paco's

Pub

Hilton Al Ain

03 768 6666

Paco's has become somewhat of a living legend thanks to the fact that it never changes. Popular because it is exactly the same now as it was when it opened in 1991, this British watering hole is a tonic for the homesick expat's soul. After a steaming plate of bangers and mash, an excellent pint of Guinness (hard to come by in these parts) and a spot of footie on the big screen, you'll almost forget you are miles away from home. There's a daily happy hour between 12:00 and 20:00.

10 Tanjore

Indian

Hotel InterContinental Al Ain

03 768 6686

Tanjore is a curry lover's dream. The menu is varied enough to please the most demanding of tastes, and provides crystal-clear descriptions and guidance on what's hot, hotter, healthy and vegetarian. The rich atmosphere and surroundings complement the delicious and tantalising flavours, and the service is what you would expect from a five-star hotel.

11 Trader Vic's

Polynesian

Al Ain Rotana Hotel

03 751 5111

Forget the desert and spend an evening in tropical island mode at this popular Polynesian venue. The menu forgoes authentic Polynesian food, preferring instead to satisfy the cosmopolitan clientele with a delicious and diverse range of international dishes. The wine list is extensive, albeit somewhat overshadowed by the impressive list of cocktails, some of which are so potent they should carry a health warning!

12 The Wok

Far Eastern

Al Ain InterContinental Hotel

03 768 6686

Staff members here are proud of their food, service and reputation, and with good reason – The Wok is one of the better restaurants serving Far Eastern cuisine in the area. Set in the landscaped grounds of the hotel, the ambience here is quiet and relaxed with soft background music and stylish decor. The Wok is popular and reservations are essential, particularly for the outstanding seafood buffet on Sunday nights.

Visitor Info

Entering Abu Dhabi

ABU DHABI IS AN OPEN-MINDED AND HOSPITABLE SOCIETY AND VISITORS ARE MADE TO FEEL BOTH WELCOME AND SAFE.

All visitors to Abu Dhabi, except for citizens of the Gulf Co-operation Council (GCC states), will require a visa. However, certain nationalities automatically gain a visit visa on arrival, usually for 60 days and then they can renew their visa once for an additional period of 30 days (for a fee of Dhs.500). Citizens of **Andorra, Australia, Austria, Brunei, Belgium, Canada, Denmark, Finland, France, Germany, Greece, Hong Kong, Iceland, Ireland, Italy, Japan, Liechtenstein, Luxembourg, Malaysia, Monaco, the Netherlands, New Zealand, Norway, Portugal, San Marino, Singapore, South Korea, Spain, Sweden, Switzerland, United Kingdom, United States of America, and Vatican City** receive an automatic visa on arrival in Abu Dhabi. If you are not one of these nationalities then your hotel can take care of the paperwork for you. You will need to provide them with a passport copy and the fee, which is usually around Dhs.200 per visa. If you have left things until the last minute, your hotel can arrange an emergency visa for you (usually ready within 24 hours), but this will cost an additional Dhs.100. Once this visa is approved it will be deposited at the airport for you to collect on arrival. For those travelling onwards to a destination other than that of their original departure, a special transit visa (up to 96 hours) may be obtained free of charge through any airline carrier operating in the UAE.

There is no customs duty levied on personal effects entering Abu Dhabi. It is forbidden, however, to import drugs and pornographic items. Once you have collected your bags in the arrivals hall at Abu Dhabi International Airport, they are x-rayed; CDs, DVDs, videos, books, and magazines may be checked with a more thorough eye than in other countries, and suspect items, particularly movies, may be temporarily confiscated for the material to be approved. Unless it's offensive, it may be collected at a later date. Both arriving and departing passengers have access to the Duty Free area.

There are currently no restrictions on the import/export of local or foreign currency. The UAE is party to international agreements on money laundering. A new anti money laundering law not only penalises individuals who violate the law, but also financial institutions. The penalty for money laundering is a prison sentence of up to seven years or a maximum fine of Dhs.300,000. The limit for undeclared cash that you can carry with you into the country is Dhs.40,000.

Airport

Abu Dhabi International Airport is undergoing a major expansion and redevelopment programme. The aircraft gates at the existing terminal are arranged around a circular satellite, so you won't have to walk far to reach immigration and the baggage reclaim area. If you haven't arranged a hotel limousine pick up or hire car, a taxi to the city centre will cost about Dh65.

Duty Free Allowances:

- **Cigarettes – 2,000**
- **Cigars – 400**
- **Tobacco – 2 kg**
- **Alcohol (non-Muslim adults only) – two litres of spirits and two litres of wine**

Travel Facts

AS A GUEST IN ABU DHABI YOU WILL BE VERY WELL LOOKED AFTER. THE UAE IS TOLERANT, LIBERAL AND FORWARD THINKING IN ITS REGULATIONS. YOU CAN EXPECT NOTHING LESS THAN EXEMPLARY HOSPITALITY.

Banks & ATMS

There is a huge network of local and international banks strictly controlled by the UAE Central Bank. Hours are Saturday to Wednesday, 08:00 – 13:00 (some open 16:30 – 18:30) and Thursday, 08:00 – 12:00. Practically all banks operate ATMs accepting a range of cards. For non-UAE based cards, the exchange rates used in the transaction are normally extremely competitive and the process is faster and far less hassle than using traditional travellers' cheques. ATMs can be found in the airport, most shopping malls, and hotels as well as the occasional petrol station.

Credit Cards

Most shops, hotels and restaurants accept the major credit cards (these being American Express, Diners Club, MasterCard and Visa). Smaller retailers are sometimes less keen to accept credit cards and you may have to pay an extra 5% for processing. If you wish, you can call your local credit card company to complain if you are charged this 5% 'fee'. Conversely, paying in cash might mean a discount – so ask. Cash is always your best option in the souks, unless buying expensive jewellery.

Currency

The monetary unit is the dirham (Dhs.) which has been tied to the US dollar since 1980. Each dirham divides into 100 fils. Coin denominations are Dhs.1, 50 fils, 25 fils 10 fils and 5 fils (although the latter two are very rare). Notes come in Dhs.5, 10, 20, 50, 100, 200, 500 and 1,000. As of October 2007 the exchange rates stood at around 3.67 to the US dollar, 5.20 to the euro and 7.50 to the UK pound.

Disabled Visitors

Abu Dhabi International Airport and many of the five-star hotels have wheelchair facilities. Elsewhere, such facilities are still somewhat limited, even at tourist attractions, though the situation is improving. In some places wheelchair access is by delivery ramp, hence the gradient may be steep.

Dress

Lightweight summer clothing is suitable for most of the year, but something slightly warmer may be needed for the winter months. Be sure to take a jacket or sweater when visiting hotels or the cinema, as the air conditioning can be excessive. Bikinis and short shorts are perfectly acceptable on the beach or by the pool. But context is important. Visitors should respect Muslim sensibilities by not wearing excessively revealing clothing around town, and especially not during Ramadan.

Electricity & Water

Electricity and water services in Abu Dhabi are excellent and power cuts or water shortages are practically unheard of. The electricity supply is 220/240 volts and 50 cycles. Sockets are mostly three pin, but some are two pin. The tap water is heavily purified and safe to drink, but most people prefer to drink locally bottled mineral water or international brands.

Female Visitors

Women visitors should not face any problems while in Abu Dhabi. Of course, as noted above, it helps to avoid wearing tight or revealing clothing and to ignore the occasional unwanted stares, particularly on the public beaches, you'll save yourself some aggravation.

Go Mobile

Ahlan is a new service being offered to short-term visitors by Etisalat at their counters or payment machines. The Dhs.90 package provides a local mobile phone number for 90 days. The first three-minute international call, 90 minutes of local talk time and nine national or international SMS messages are free. If you dial a local landline from an international mobile you will have to dial 009712 before the number.

Health Requirements

Unless you have recently been in an area where you could have been exposed to cholera or yellow fever, there is no need to get a health certificate before you enter Abu Dhabi. Restrictions do change though, so it is better to check before you travel (see the World Health Organisation website at www.who.int/ith/en). There is no risk of getting malaria in the city of Abu Dhabi. However, be warned that the malaria-carrying mosquito has on rare occasions been encountered in the mountains of the UAE.

In an Emergency

Police: Abu Dhabi is among the safest and most crime-free places in the world. Despite this, accidents and bad things do still happen. The police here are respected, involved in the community and very approachable. They are also easily recognisable in their ash grey uniforms. In an emergency, call 999.

Lost/stolen Property: If any valuables go missing, check with your hotel first, or if you've lost something in a taxi, call the taxi company's lost and found department. There are a lot of honest people in Abu Dhabi who will return found items. If you've had no luck, then call the Abu Dhabi Police to report the loss or theft; you'll be advised on the next steps to follow. Also make sure you keep a passport photocopy in a secure place to avoid hassle should you misplace it. If you do lose your passport, however, your next stop should be your embassy or consulate.

Hospitals And Healthcare: The quality of medical care in Abu Dhabi is generally regarded as being excellent and visitors should have little trouble obtaining appropriate treatment, whether privately or, in case of an emergency, from the government run hospitals. You can reach emergency services by dialling 999.

Car Accidents: While the infrastructure is superb, the general standard of driving is not and traffic accidents are unfortunately plentiful. Should you find yourself in such an unfortunate situation, get everyone to safety, call the police on 999 and await their instructions.

Mobile phones

Etisalat has over 60 reciprocal agreements with countries for roaming services, allowing visitors, whose countries are part of the agreement, to use their mobile in the UAE. Etisalat also offers a useful prepaid service called 'Wasel'. Purchase a SIM card and a local number is supplied. Calls are charged at the local UAE rate. Find out more about Etisalat's services on www.e4me.ae. Du is a new network which offers similar services to Etisalat and you can purchase a pay-as-you-go SIM card when you present your visitor visa at one of their outlets. For more information visit www.du.ae.

Money Exchanges

Money exchanges are available all over Abu Dhabi, they offer good service and reasonable exchange rates that are often better than the banks. Many hotels will also exchange money and travellers' cheques at the standard (poor) hotel rate. Be aware that they tend to close between 13:00 and 16:30.

Pharmacies

Abu Dhabi's pharmacies are well stocked with all the medications you are likely to need and many items are available over the counter without prescription. At least one pharmacy in the city will stay open 24 hours. Call 677 7929 for the location. There is also a pharmacy attached to Ahalia Hospital (626 2666) that is open around the clock.

Photography

While normal tourist photography is acceptable, it is polite to ask permission before taking photos of people, particularly women. In general, photographs of government buildings, military installations, ports and airports should not be taken and cameras may be banned in some public areas.

Time

Local time in Abu Dhabi is +4hrs UCT (Universal Co-ordinated Time, formerly GMT) with no summer saving time and so no clock changes. Evenings are busy early on with families and late into the night with party-goers.

Tipping

Tipping practices are similar to most parts of the world. A number of restaurants include service, although it is unlikely to end up with your waiter; otherwise, 10% is normal. If you tip a taxi driver, round up to the nearest Dhs.5 or Dhs.10.

Travel Insurance

It is always a good idea to get travel insurance. Choose a reputable insurer and take your time to pick a plan that will cover the activities you intend to enjoy in Abu Dhabi, especially if these include extreme sports such as quad biking or diving.

Travelling With Children

Abu Dhabi is a family friendly destination. Parks, amusement centres and beaches abound. Hotels and shopping malls are well geared up for children, offering everything from babysitting services to kids' activities. Restaurants, on the other hand, may have children's menus but tend not to have many high chairs so be sure to ask when you book. Discounted rates for children are common, even if they aren't displayed.

Public Holiday	Date
New Year's Day	Jan 1 – Fixed
Al Hijra (Islamic) New Year	Jan 10 2008 – Moon
Prophet Mohammed's Birthday	Mar 20 2008 – Moon
Accession Day	Aug 6 – (tbc)
Lailat Al Miraj	Aug 22 2007 – Moon
Lailat Al Miraj	Sept 1 2007 – Moon
Ramadan Begins	Sept 13 2007 – Moon
Eid Al Fitr	Oct 22 2007 – Moon
National Day	Dec 2 – Fixed
UAE National Day	Dec 2 – Fixed
Eid Al Adha	Dec 20 2007 – Moon

Websites	Information
www.abudhabitourism.ae	Abu Dhabi Tourism Authority
www.exploreabudhabi.ae	Abu Dhabi Tourism Authority
www.alain.ae	Abu Dhabi Tourism Authority
www.uaeinteract.com	UAE government official news and information
www.adcci-uae.com	Chamber of Commerce and Industry
www.adiamet.gov.ae	Weather office
www.adpolice.gov.ae	Abu Dhabi police
www.auhcustoms.gov.ae	Abu Dhabi customs
www.du.ae	Telephone service provider
www.embassyworld.com	Embassies abroad
www.etihadairways.com	Etihad Airways
www.etisalat.ae	Telephone service provider
www.gulfnews.com	Online UAE newspaper
www.khaleejtimes.com	Online UAE newspaper
www.ameinfo.com	Middle East news site

Basic Arabic

English	Arabic
Accident	Haadith
Insurance	ta'miyn
Papers	waraq
Permit/licence	rukhsaa
Police	al shurtaa
Sorry	aasif(m)/aasifa (f)
God willing	in shaa'a l-laah
No	la
Please	min fadlak (m)/min fadliki(f)
Thank you	shukran
Yes	na'am
Greeting (peace be upon you)	as-salaamu alaykom
Hello (in reply)	marhabtayn
Hello	marhaba
How are you?	kayf haalak(m)/kayf haalik(f)
My name is...	ismiy…
What is your name?	shuw ismak(m)/shuw ismik(f)
Airport	mataar
East	sharq
Hotel	funduq
Left	yassar
Right	yamiyn
Restaurant	mata'am
Sea/beach	il bahar
Slow Down	schway schway
South	januwb
Stop	kuf
Straight ahead	siydaa

Getting Around

ABU DHABI IS COMPACT, WELL LAID OUT AND AN EASY CITY TO NAVIGATE. WHILE PUBLIC TRANSPORT IS LIMITED THERE ARE MORE THAN ENOUGH ALTERNATIVES TO MAKE TRAVELLING EASY AND ENJOYABLE.

Taxi

By far the most common method of getting around is by taxi. These are reasonably priced, plentiful and can be flagged down at the roadside. Most drivers have a passable understanding of English and are familiar with the popular tourist destinations. The more upmarket Al Ghazal or NTC taxis must be booked by phone (by dialling 444 7787 or 622 3300).

Car Hire

You will find all the major international car rental companies in Abu Dhabi, plus a number of local firms. It is best to shop around as rates can vary considerably. Still, it's worth remembering that the larger, more reputable firms generally have more reliable vehicles and a greater capacity to help in an emergency.

Bus

The Abu Dhabi Municipality operates bus routes all over the emirate, as well as in the city. Attempts are being made to make the service more cost effective and organised, with more readily available route information and timetables. The service operates more or less around the clock and fares are inexpensive – as little as Dhs.1 for travel within the capital. For more information, contact Abu Dhabi Transport (02 443 1500).

Boat

Various companies offer trips by dhow, or motor boat, to explore the islands off the coast; alternatively you can try hiring a fishing boat to do this privately. A water taxi ('abra') service is planned for the new Al Raha Beach development, which will link Abu Dhabi Island, Saadiyat Island and on towards the Abu Dhabi International Airport.

Walking & Cycling

Cities in the UAE are generally very car orientated and not designed to encourage walking, especially as daytime temperatures in the summer months reach around 45°C. That said, the relative compactness of Abu Dhabi's main area makes walking a pleasant way of getting around in the cooler months, and an evening stroll along the corniche is a must. Similarly, cycling is not common and therefore a little dangerous, although there is a safe cycle track at the corniche.

Car Rental Agencies

Abu Dhabi Rent a Car		02 644 3770
Avis Rent a Car	Abu Dhabi	02 575 7180
	Al Ain	03 768 7262
Budget Rent-A-Car		02 633 4200
Diamond Lease		02 622 2028
Europcar	Abu Dhabi	02 626 1441
	Al Ain	03 721 0180
Hertz Rent A Car		02 672 0060
Thrifty	Abu Dhabi	02 575 7400
	Al Ain	03 754 5711
United Car Rentals		02 642 2203

Annual Events

THROUGHOUT THE YEAR ABU DHABI HOSTS A NUMBER OF MAJOR ANNUAL EVENTS WHICH ATTRACT VISITORS FROM FAR AND WIDE. THE EVENTS LISTED BELOW ARE SOME OF THE MORE POPULAR FIXTURES ON THE SOCIAL CALENDAR AND ARE WELL WORTH ADDING TO YOUR HOLIDAY ITINERARY.

Abu Dhabi Golf Championship — January

www.abudhabigolfchampionship.com

The Championship puts Abu Dhabi into the international golfing spotlight as the first European PGA Tour ranking event of the calendar year. Launched in January 2006, the Championship has already become extremely popular. It was won by Paul Casey in 2007, and has featured leading players such as Thomas Bjorn, Sergio Garcia, V J Singh, John Daly and Colin Montgomerie, with Chris Dimarco running away with the prize after a fantastic display.

Al Ain Aerobatic Show — January

www.alainaerobaticshow.com

This international event attracts top aerobatics teams from around the world. Held at the airport just outside Al Ain, the show has a festival atmosphere with tents and displays related to flying, aerobatics and stunt flying. Abu Dhabi corniche is the venue for one of the international series of Red Bull Air Races, an exciting competition in which the world's most talented pilots display their skills.

Dhow Racing

April-September

www.emirates-heritageclub.com

Traditional wooden dhows of 40 to 60 feet in length present a majestic sight when powered along by up to 100 men with the help of the wind. Scheduled dhow races take place throughout the year, mostly between September and April. The ones held off Abu Dhabi are short coastal races and the boats, many of which are old pearling vessels, have a shallow draught ideal for sailing closer to the corniche.

Abu Dhabi Classic Car Rally

February

www.abudhabiclassic.com

Under the Patronage of H.H. Sheikh Sultan Bin Tahnoon Al Nahyan, this new event brings the best in classic car racing to the emirate. Alongside the FIA European Championship Rally, there will be a street festival with food, entertainment and activities for kids.

Terry Fox Run

February

www.terryfoxrun.org

Every year, thousands of people around the world run, jog, walk, cycle and even rollerblade their way around a designated course to raise money for cancer research programmes. The Abu Dhabi route is eight kilometres along the corniche and usually takes place in February. For more information, check the local media, or contact the Ambassador's Office, Canadian Embassy (02 407 1300).

Exhibitions & Conferences — Various

www.adnec.ae

Abu Dhabi is rapidly becoming one of the world leading venues for business events, hosting a growing calendar of international exhibitions and conferences throughout the year. Many visitors choose to combine business with pleasure by scheduling a holiday around such events. Among the best known are IDEX (the International Defence Exhibition and Conference), ADIPEX (Abu Dhabi International Petroleum Exhibition) and GIBTM (the Gulf Incentive, Business Travel & Meetings exhibition).

Abu Dhabi Classical Music Festival — March

www.adconcert.com

The Abu Dhabi Classical Music Festival, organised by the Abu Dhabi Music & Arts Foundation (ADMAF), will showcase the best in classical music, drawing on local talent as well as renowned musicians from overseas. Highlights of the ADMAF's programme in 2007 included a performance by the European Fine Arts Trio.

Red Bull Air Race — April

and www.redbullairrace.com

The Air Race, under the patronage of HH Sheikh Hazza Bin Zayed Al Nahyan, brings the Red Bull Air Race World Series to the UAE capital, the first of eight rounds in eight different cities around the world. Dubbed 'Formula 1 racing in the sky', the sport is the ultimate test of a pilot's skill and precision.

Tall A Sad Competition April

Al Ain is the venue for this exciting desert car competition, which has more than 30 competitors from countries in the Gulf.

Horse Racing October – April

www.adec-web.com

The Abu Dhabi Equestrian Club provides information on horse racing and show jumping. The season lasts from October to April and racing takes place every Sunday night during these months; contact ADEC (02 445 5500) or check their website for further details. For endurance events and for further details on horse racing and show jumping, log on to the UAE Equestrian and Racing Federation's website (www.uaeequafed.ae).

Powerboat Racing October – May

www.adimsc.ae

The UAE is well established on the world championship powerboat racing circuit with Formula One (onshore) in Abu

Dhabi and Class One (offshore) in Dubai and Fujairah. Abu Dhabi International Marine Sports Club has a racing calendar running from October to May and hosts the final round of the Formula One series at the end of the season.

UAE Desert Challenge November

www.uaedesertchallenge.com

This is the highest profile motor sport event in the country and is often the culmination of the cross-country rallying world cup. The event attracts some of the world's top rally drivers and bike riders who compete in the car, truck and motocross categories.

The Abu Dhabi Cycling Race of Champions November

www.abudhabiroc.com

The Abu Dhabi Cycling Race of Champions is sanctioned by UCI ProTour – run by cycling's governing body Union Cyclist International, which operates Europe's leading races: Spain's La Vuelta, Italy's Giro d'Italia, and the Tour de France. The route of the race includes a challenging mountain stage up Jebel Hafeet, the emirate's highest point at nearly 4,000 feet, flanked by two flat stages through the capital's main highways.

Formula One

Abu Dhabi has secured the right to host a Formula 1 Grand Prix from 2009. The announcement followed the success of the first Formula 1 Festival that brought the top drivers (including world champion Fernando Alonso) and their cars to the streets of Abu Dhabi in February 2007. A track is already under construction at Yas Island close to the capital.

VISITORS TO ABU DHABI CAN CHOOSE FROM INSPIRING AND LUXURIOUS HOTELS, HOTEL APARTMENTS AND EVEN ECO-TOURIST RESORTS. IF IT'S OPULENCE YOU'RE LOOKING FOR THEN YOU'VE CHOSEN THE RIGHT DESTINATION. IN FACT THERE ARE FEW PLACES IN THE WORLD THAT OFFER SUCH JAW-DROPPINGLY SPECTACULAR SURROUNDINGS.

Abu Dhabi Airport Hotel 5★

www.adddf.ae 02 575 7377

This convenient stopover hotel is a godsend for weary travellers who have long transit times at the airport. Alternatively, if you have an early morning flight, you could check in the night before and just walk to the boarding gates after having had a good night's sleep in this comfortable hotel. It has several food and beverage outlets, a health club and children's facilities.

Al Ain Palace Hotel 4★

www.alainpalacehotel.com 02 679 4777

The Al Ain Palace is one of Abu Dhabi's well-established hotels (fondly known as the 'Ally Pally'). It offers international restaurants and theme bars, 110 deluxe rooms and suites, plus self-contained studios and chalet-style rooms. Situated close to the corniche in the central business district its location is perfect for discovering Abu Dhabi and its surrounding areas.

Al Raha Beach Hotel 5★

www.ncth.com 02 508 0555

This is Abu Dhabi's first boutique resort with spacious rooms enjoying great views over the Arabian Gulf and a good selection of dining outlets. Leisure facilities at the resort include a health club and spa, indoor and outdoor pools, a gym, squash courts, watersports, and a kids' playground. Many UAE residents enjoy weekend breaks here which is always a good stamp of approval.

Armed Forces Officers Club & Hotel 5★

www.afoc.mil.ae 02 441 5900

Located near the bridges and near to the airport, this luxurious hotel has over 530 rooms and 64 suites. There are a number of food outlets, extensive recreational facilities (including swimming pools, indoor shooting galleries, a bowling alley and separate facilities for ladies), as well as children's play areas with two pools.

Beach Rotana Hotel & Towers 5★

www.rotana.com 02 644 3000

The hotel boasts a conference centre, luxury suites and 414 sea-facing rooms, and it also offers dining options to please most palates, including Polynesian and Italian. Direct access to the Abu Dhabi Mall is an added bonus. The Rotana's many leisure facilities include a long stretch of private beach, a covered children's play area, tennis and squash courts, and swimming pools.

Crowne Plaza 4★

www.ichotelsgroup.com 02 621 0000

Situated in the heart of the city and close to Abu Dhabi's shopping district and the beach, this hotel is ideal for both business and leisure travellers. The hotel has four restaurants and a bar, an onsite health and fitness centre, a rooftop pool offering stunning views of the city, 13 meeting rooms, three executive floors and an excellent business centre.

Danat Resort Jebel Dhanna 5★

www.ncth.com 02 801 2222

Danat Resort Jebel Dhanna is located 240 km west of Abu Dhabi city, within driving distance of the untouched dunes of the Arabian desert. The resort has 108 rooms, almost a kilometre of secluded beach and comprehensive leisure facilities including watersports, two floodlit tennis courts, two squash courts and a nine-hole, par 36 sand golf course and driving range.

Emirates Palace 5★

www.emiratespalace.com 02 690 9000

This Abu Dhabi landmark is the ultimate in luxury and style, with 302 rooms and 92 suites, the latest technology, sumptuous decor, 15 outstanding food outlets and seven-star service. Guests can enjoy the 1.3km stretch of private beach, two amazing swimming pools, exclusive retail outlets, a spa, tennis and squash courts, a huge marina and beautifully landscaped grounds.

Grand Continental Flamingo Hotel 5★

grand-continental-flamingo.com 02 626 2200

This small hotel is ideally situated in the centre of town close to all amenities. It has 152 rooms, all of which offer good views of the city. There are four restaurants including the popular Peppino, an Italian restaurant that draws the crowds. The Grand Continental Flamingo also has a host of handy business facilities and a well-equipped gym.

Hilton Baynunah Tower 5★

www.hilton.com 02 632 7777

Undoubtedly one of the most impressive towers on the Corniche, the 40 storey, blue-glass Hilton Baynunah Tower has the accolade of being the tallest hotel complex in Abu Dhabi. As you would expect, the comfortable rooms and suites offer breathtaking views of the coastline and the city. The hotel also has a restaurant and a health club, and an indoor pool with stunning views.

Hilton International Abu Dhabi 5★

www.hilton.com 02 681 1900

Conveniently located near Abu Dhabi's financial and business district, the Hilton has 350 beautifully decorated rooms and suites. The Hiltonia Beach Club, accessible via a pedestrian tunnel, has a private beach, swimming pools and a luxurious health club. Some Abu Dhabi favourites are here, including Hemingways, renowned Italian restaurant BiCE, and a chilled out Jazz Bar.

Le Meridien Abu Dhabi 5★

www.lemeridien-abudhabi.com 02 644 6666

Recently renovated, this hotel is set in tranquil landscaped gardens and has plenty of leisure facilities and activities to satisfy all tastes. There is a private beach, two swimming pools (plus a separate kids' pool), a health club with state-of-the-art equipment and a splendid spa. Perhaps most impressive is the hotel's collection of 15 renowned food and beverage outlets.

InterContinental Abu Dhabi 5★

www.ichotelsgroup.com 02 666 6888

Major renovations have seen the InterContinental regain its place as one of the emirate's more impressive five-star hotels. There's a range of high-end restaurants offering Thai, Brazilian and Italian cuisine. Excellent facilities include a private beach, outdoor pool, 24 hour gym, and the largest lounge in Abu Dhabi, located on the top floor of the hotel.

Le Royal Meridien Abu Dhabi 5★

www.lemeridien.com 02 674 2020

This landmark hotel has 265 beautiful rooms and suites, most of which have excellent views over the corniche and out to sea. There are 13 excellent food and beverage outlets, most noteworthy are Al Fanar, the revolving rooftop restaurant, and the Shuja Yacht, upon which you can take a romantic dinner cruise. Leisure facilities include indoor and outdoor swimming pools and a fitness centre.

Liwa Hotel 4★

www.ncth.com 02 882 2000

The beauty of this hotel is its breathtaking location – situated in the heart of the desert and surrounded by impressive sand dunes and overlooking one of the largest oases in Arabia. With 66 rooms, two restaurants, a swimming pool with separate children's pool and tranquil landscaped gardens, the Liwa Hotel has become a popular retreat.

Mafraq Hotel 4★

www.ncth.com 02 582 2666

Built in 1996, and conveniently located 10 minutes from Abu Dhabi International Airport and 20 minutes from the city centre, this quiet hotel features 120 rooms and four suites in relaxed, landscaped surroundings, and a decent range of good-value restaurants. There is also an internet cafe, barber and gift shop at the hotel in addition to a wide range of sports facilities.

Mercure Grand Jebel Hafeet 5★

www.mercure.com 03 783 8888

Its precarious location on Jebel Hafeet makes the Mercure Grand a unique hotel. It is situated just two kilometres from the summit and offers breathtaking views and clean mountain air. The hotel includes a gym, a spa, a fantastic pool as well as a play area. Diners at Le Belvedere can admire stunning vistas of the city at night, as can those out for a stroll through the hotel gardens.

Millennium Hotel 5★

www.milleniumhotels.com 02 626 2700

This modern hotel near the corniche has great views across the city. It has 325 elegantly decorated rooms and three restaurants serving Moroccan, Italian and international cuisine. It is home to renowned champagne and cigar bar, Cristal. The hotel has great business and leisure facilities, including boardrooms, a business centre and Le Club luxury health and fitness club.

Shangri-La Hotel Qaryat Al Beri 5★

www.shangri-la.com 02 509 8888

This new resort lies on a one kilometre stretch of beach between Abu Dhabi's gateway bridges, Al Maqta and Al Mussafah and will eventually cover 8.5 hectares and have 214 rooms and suites. The first phase boasts a three-storey spa, an impressive number of retail outlets and a waterway, complete with abras.

Sheraton Abu Dhabi 5★

www.sheraton.com/abudhabi 02 677 3333

Situated on the beautifully revamped area of the corniche, the Sheraton is a favourite for business and leisure travellers. The hotel has 272 rooms, many with sea views, and 12 dining and drinking outlets including the popular Italian restaurant La Mamma. Leisure activities include outdoor heated pools (with separate kids' pool), a fitness centre and a private beach offering watersports.

Sheraton Khalidiya Hotel 5★

www.sheraton.com 02 666 6220

Sheraton Khalidiya has just had a complete refurbishment, creating a world of style and comfort. The hotel is located in the centre of the business district, close to ministries, embassies and shopping centers and is only 32 kilometers away from the airport. It has 195 luxurious guest rooms and suites, ideally designed for business and leisure travellers.

Al Ain Rotana Hotel 5★

www.rotana.com 03 754 5111

Set in the heart of the garden city, this hotel allows easy access to Al Ain's tourist attractions. The 100 spacious rooms, suites and chalets are comfortable and offer a wonderful base from which to explore Al Ain. The hotel has a Bodylines Fitness Centre, an outdoor pool and six dining and entertainment outlets including the Polynesian restaurant Trader Vic's which is always busy.

Hilton Al Ain 5★

www.hilton.com 03 768 6666

Near the heart of Al Ain, this hotel, built in 1971, is a great place to stay while exploring the many attractions of the green city (such as the zoo, the museum, Jebel Hafeet and the Hili Tombs). The 202 guestrooms, suites and villas all look over landscaped gardens, and there are five bars and restaurants, floodlit tennis/squash courts, health club and a nine-hole golf course.

Hotel InterContinental Al Ain 5★

www.interconti.com 03 768 6686

Landscaped gardens, swimming pools, guestrooms, a fitness centre, special activities for children, seven food and beverage outlets, deluxe villas and a Royal Villa with private Jacuzzi all combine to make this a great leisure retreat. This is one of the undisputed hotspots for socialising in Al Ain.

Hotel Apartments

A cheaper alternative to staying in a hotel is to rent furnished accommodation on a daily, weekly, monthly or yearly basis. One advantage is that the place can feel far more like a home than a hotel room. Usually the apartments will come fully furnished and have a maid service.

Hotel	Number	Website	Star Ratir
Ain Al Fayda	03 783 8333		3
Al Diar Mina Hotel	02 678 1000	www.aldiarhotels.com	3
International Rotana Inn	02 677 9900	www.rotana.com	3
Saba Hotel	02 644 8333	www.ramee-group.com	3
Zakher Hotel	02 627 5300	www.uaeyha.com	3
Al Maha Rotana Suites	02 610 6666	www.rotana.com	Apar
Al Rawda Rotana Suites	02 445 7111	www.rotana.com	Apar
Hilton Corniche Residence	02 627 6000	www.hilton.com	Apar
Oasis Residence	02 641 7000		Apar
Vision Hotel Apartments	02 699 2666	www.visionhotel.net	Apar

Explorer Products

Residents' Guides

All you need to know about living, working and enjoying life in these exciting destinations

* Covers not final: titles released second quarter 2008

Mini Guides

Perfect pocket-sized visitors' guides

*

*

*

Activity Guides

Drive, trek, dive and swim... life will never be boring again

Mini Maps

Fit the city in your pocket

Maps

Wherever you are, never get lost again

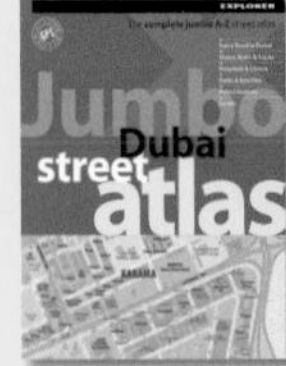

* Covers not final; titles released second quarter 2008

Photography Books

Beautiful cities caught through the lens.

Lifestyle Products & Calendars

The perfect accessories for a buzzing lifestyle

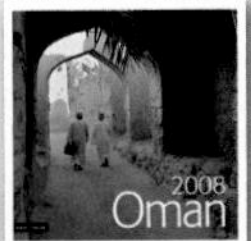

Explorer Team

Publisher
Alistair MacKenzie
Associate Publisher Claire England

Editorial
Group Editor Jane Roberts
Lead Editors David Quinn, Matt Farquharson, Sean Kearns, Tim Binks, Tom Jordan
Deputy Editors Helen Spearman, Jakob Marsico, Katie Drynan, Pamela Afram, Richard Greig, Tracy Fitzgerald
Senior Editorial Assistant Mimi Stankova
Editorial Assistants Grace Carnay, Ingrid Cupido, Kathryn Calderon

Design
Creative Director Pete Maloney
Art Director Ieyad Charaf
Design Manager Alex Jeffries
Senior Designer Iain Young
Layout Manager Jayde Fernandes
Designers Hashim Moideen, Rafi Pullat, Shawn Jackson Zuzarte
Cartography Manager Zainudheen Madathil
Cartographers Noushad Madathil, Sunita Lakhiani
Design Admin Manager Shyrell Tamayo
Production Coordinator Maricar Ong

Photography
Photography Manager Pamela Grist
Photographer Victor Romero
Image Editor Henry Hilos

Sales & Marketing
Media Sales Area Managers Laura Zuffa, Stephen Jones
GCC Retail Sales Manager Michael Dominic
Global Partners Sales Manager Andrew Burgess
Corporate Sales Executive Ben Merrett
Marketing Manager Kate Fox
Marketing Executive Annabel Clough
Digital Content Manager Derrick Pereira
International Retail Sales Manager Ivan Rodrigues
Retail Sales Coordinator Kiran Melwani
Retail Sales Supervisor Mathew Samuel
Retail Sales Merchandisers Johny Mathew, Shan Kumar
Sales & Marketing Coordinator Lennie Mangalino
Distribution Executives Ahmed Mainodin, Firos Khan, Mannie Lugtu
Warehouse Assistants Mohammed Kunjaymo, Najumudeen K.I.
Drivers Mohammed Sameer, Shabsir Madathil

Finance & Administration
Finance Manager Michael Samuel
HR & Administration Manager Andrea Fust
Junior Accountant Cherry Enriquez
Accounts Assistant Darwin Lovitos
Administrators Enrico Maullon, Joy Tuborg, Kelly Tesoro
Driver Rafi Jamal

IT
IT Administrator Ajay Krishnan
Senior Software Engineer Bahrudeen Abdul
Software Engineer Roshni Ahuja

Contact Us

Reader Response

If you have any comments and suggestions, fill out our online reader response form and you could win prizes. Log on to **www.explorerpublishing.com**

General Enquiries

We'd love to hear your thoughts and answer any questions you have about this book or any other Explorer product. Contact us at **Info@explorerpublishing.com**

Careers

If you fancy yourself as an Explorer, send your CV (stating the position you're interested in) to **Jobs@explorerpublishing.com**

Designlab and Contract Publishing

For enquiries about Explorer's Contract Publishing arm and design services contact **Designlab@explorerpublishing.com**

Maps

For cartography enquries, including orders and comments, contact **Maps@explorerpublishing.com**

Corporate Sales

For bulk sales and customisation options, for this book or any Explorer product, contact **Sales@explorerpublishing.com**

Index

#

A

B

C

D

E

F

G

H

I

J

K

L

M

N

O

P

Q

R

S

T

U

V

W

Z

Notes

Notes